Dear Susan,

read now!

Molly

Happy

Return!

Susan Bork

HOW TO MAKE MONEY
USING OTHER PEOPLE'S MONEY

HOW TO MAKE MONEY USING OTHER PEOPLE'S MONEY

SUSAN BONDY

THE BOBBS-MERRILL COMPANY, INC.
Indianapolis/New York

Published by The Bobbs-Merrill Company, Inc.
Indianapolis   New York

Library of Congress Cataloging in Publication Data

Bondy, Susan.
　Other people's money.

　Includes index.
1. Investments　　　I. Title.
HG4521.B623　　　332.6'78　　　　81-18185
　　　　　　　　　　　　　　　　　　　AACR2
ISBN 0-672-52702-2

Designed by Jacques Chazaud
Manufactured in the United States of America

First printing

To my Mother and Father, who helped me to understand
the importance of planning and learning:

Planning for a year?
sow rice . . .

Planning for a decade?
plant trees . . .

Planning for a lifetime?
educate the person.

ACKNOWLEDGMENTS

I am indebted to a number of people whose help and encouragement made this book possible.

Warm thanks to:

    Bill Adler, my agent, for his guidance.

    Roger Draper, who showed me the skills of writing.

    Barbara Lagowski for her editorial contributions.

    Doe Lang for her love, her support, and her belief in me.

Special thanks is due to those friends and colleagues who read the original manuscript for accuracy, continuity, and clarity: Scott Higgins, Linda Margolin, Susan Fisher, Ed Bondy (my father), and especially H. F. Moody, Jr., who managed to take time out during an especially busy period.

Thanks also to all those whose comments, suggestions, or facts enhanced the script, and to the lawyers, accountants, bankers, insurance experts, and investment professionals who provided answers to my many questions.

CONTENTS

SECTION I:
MAKING MONEY WITH MONEY

You're Richer Than You Think

One evening about a year ago I had dinner at the home of my friends Fred and Margo Cooper (not their real names). Margo is an executive secretary in a large corporation, and Fred is a design engineer with another industrial giant. They live with their two children in a nice house on a nice street in a nice town that is worthy of their $50,000-a-year joint income.

The Coopers' home is filled with appliances and gadgets; they appear to have "the good life." Yet Margo and Fred were worried about money.

"Fifty thousand may sound like a lot," Margo started off, "but of course Uncle Sam takes about 30 percent of it before we even see a penny. And the bank gets an additional 25 percent for the mortgage."

"We've got a few hundred dollars in the bank," Fred added, "but the interest we earn on it is so much lower than inflation that we're *losing* money, not making it. And to tell you the truth, in the last year or so we haven't saved a cent."

Margo and Fred were right: they did have a money problem. However, the problem wasn't a lack of money, but a lack of knowledge about money. *And* about credit *and* about insurance *and* about investments.

Both of them knew quite well that my business was giving financial advice, but they also knew that I gave it to big corporations because they were willing to pay for it. What they did not realize was that anyone can benefit from financial advice, often the very same advice that the biggest companies get.

Do you still have doubts? So did the Coopers until I explained it to them.

Margo and Fred thought their only financial resources were their salaries — which they spent to the hilt — and their bank account, with its unimpressive balance. But when I started asking questions I found out that Margo, through her employer, had a life insurance policy worth $32,000, and that Fred, through his, had accumulated a $54,000 profit-sharing fund. "So what?" asked Margo. "We can't do anything with that money."

And at that point they were *not* doing anything with it. Money that could have been making money for them was making money for someone else instead.

What Margo and Fred still did not know — and what most people don't — is that it is possible to make money by borrowing against a life insurance policy or a profit-sharing fund, or against other such assets, at low rates of interest and investing this money at higher rates of interest.

Margo could have borrowed up to 100 percent of the cash value of her life insurance policy at 8 percent interest, and Fred could have borrowed up to 75 percent of his profit-sharing fund at 12 percent. At the time, banks were charging about 20 percent for personal loans. The low rates were available to the Coopers because the insurance underwriters had set the rate years earlier and were not allowed to increase it for policies already in effect; as for the profit-sharing plan, low interest on loans was an extra benefit to members.

"So what?" they asked again. "That's 8 percent and 12 percent interest that we can't afford. We would simply be adding to our expenses."

But they *could* afford to pay the interest. In fact, they could pay the interest and have enough money left to make a nice profit for themselves.

I suggested that Margo and Fred borrow the $32,000 at 8 percent interest from the life insurance company and $40,000 at 12 percent interest from the profit-sharing account, then take all that money to a bank and use it to purchase a certificate of deposit (CD). A CD allows the bank to use your money for a fixed period of time, usually six months or a year, for a fixed rate of interest. Guaranteed CD interest rates of 15 percent, 16 percent, even 18 percent are not uncommon. Now, Margo and Fred would be paying the life insurance company 8 percent a year, or $2,560, to borrow $32,000; and they would be paying the profit-sharing account 12 percent interest, or $4,800, to borrow $40,000. The total cost of borrowing the $72,000 would come to $7,360, which would be fully deductible from their income tax. If they invested that very same $72,000 at 18 percent, they would earn $12,960 from the bank. When they subtracted their cost ($7,360) from their earnings ($12,960), they would have gained $5,600 in pretax profit.

They had just learned one of the tricks the rich use to get richer. There are many other ways, too, and you do not have to be rich to use them.

After listening to my explanation, Margo and Fred did indeed borrow and invest the $72,000, and they did make the $5,600, and they plan to go on borrowing and investing.

Let's look at the $5,600 profit a little more closely. First, it was "found money," like money picked up in the street. Margo and Fred did not have to use their own money to make it. Every cent had been borrowed.

Second, the $5,600 was not a paper profit. It was real money, U.S. legal tender that Margo and Fred could and did hold in their hands to spend, save, and invest.

Third, they made the $5,600 without having to speculate in stocks, bonds, real estate, commodities, or anything else. They made their profit without taking any risk at all, because they invested in a federally insured certificate of deposit.

And fourth, the plan took only about fifteen minutes to absorb and about an hour to execute. Sure, they would have to pay income tax on the interest earned, but the interest they paid out was entirely tax deductible, which greatly reduced that tax bite.

The advice that helped Margo and Fred to make money from

money was not magic. There are a lot of rich people in this country, and it is not magic that has made them rich; it is sound information about money. Information available to only a few.

Why only a few? For one thing, because our educational system teaches us nothing about money matters. Sure, we learn to add and subtract. Some of us even learn how to balance a checkbook and fill out a Form 1040. But we never learn how to *really* make money.

But suppose you want to learn; where do you go? Unless you are worth a quarter of a million dollars or more, banks are not interested in advising you about how to make money. Insurance companies give plenty of advice on estate planning, but they may load you up with more insurance than you need. Stockbrokers love to tell you about stocks, bonds, and tax shelters; but what if stocks, bonds, and tax shelters aren't for you? None of this advice is necessarily bad, but it is not necessarily good either. It simply may not be right for your particular needs and circumstances.

That is where this book comes in. After that dinner with the Coopers, I realized there are lots of Margos and Freds in this country — people with assets and borrowing power but little knowledge of how to use them, or even of their existence. Nearly everyone can make money safely, quickly, simply, and legally by following the same real-life strategies the rich use to get richer. And these strategies are not pipe dreams.

No matter how much or how little money you earn, you can earn even more through investments and cost savings. And I am not talking about complicated deals. I am talking about simple and in many cases riskless investment strategies that take very little time to carry out. All you need is the ability to add, subtract, divide, and multiply, and to do simple bookkeeping. And I supply all the basics, including the arithmetic.

When you finish this book, you will have a firm grasp on how to keep more of your earnings and how to increase your net worth as well as your savings.

Why Use Other People's Money?

You'll recall that Margo and Fred did not take the money *out* of their life insurance policy and profit-sharing account; they borrowed against it. Why did I advise them to borrow instead of withdrawing their own money?

Eat Your Cake and Have It Too

First of all, a life insurance policy and a profit-sharing account are useful assets to own; and Margo and Fred were able to benefit by borrowing against them without relinquishing them. Borrowing permitted them to invest and to profit from money that was already working for them on its own account.

Opportunities from Overregulation

The second reason is that borrowing helped Margo and Fred take advantage of one of the many riskless investment opportunities that have been created by the overregulation of our money institutions. The life insurance company lent Margo and Fred money at 8 percent interest because it was obliged to do so by law. This feature had been part of the original insurance contract.

Corporations, banks, money market funds, and the federal government are currently all competing for our dollars, and the competition is so fierce that each side is offering more and more. Investors should put their money into those instruments that offer the highest yields. And if, to do so, you can borrow from sources that still charge low rates, you will end up way ahead of the game.

Leverage

Another reason for borrowing is that it can help you earn more than you could make by using only your own money. The power to make bigger profits through borrowing is called *leverage*. Let me give you an example from my own career. I once worked for a Wall Street investment banking firm. When I was asked to become a partner in the firm, I was offered stock at the market price, $20 per share, for 1,000 shares. I was to put down 10 percent, or $2,000. I got a loan for the balance, $18,000, at the current rate of 10 percent. At the end of that year I decided to leave that firm and start my own company. So I had to sell my stock back to the company. The stock was then selling at $25 a share, $5 more than I had paid for it.

When I sold my shares, I realized $25,000. With $18,000 I repaid my loan; that left $7,000. Out of that sum, I paid $1,800 in interest for the loan. That left $5,200, from which I subtracted the $2,000 down payment I had made from my own funds. From the remaining $3,200, I subtracted the $200 I could have earned in interest on the $2,000 down payment, since back then a certificate of deposit would have paid about 10 percent. (This $200 is called the *opportunity cost* of the investment.) So I found in the end that my "after-opportunity cost" profit was $3,000. I had earned a 150 percent return on my initial $2,000 investment, over and above the 10 percent my money could have earned in a CD, and all in one year.

Had I bought the stock entirely with my own money, the return on my investment would have been much less impressive. I would still have netted $25,000 from the sale of 1,000 shares at $25 each. Minus $20,000 of my initial investment, I would have been left with $5,000 profit. Minus $2,000 — my opportunity cost for having tied up $20,000 for one year — I am left again with $3,000. But that $3,000 is the return on the full $20,000, so I would have earned only 15 percent on $20,000. Versus 150 percent on $2,000. That is the power of leverage.

What happens to money when you leverage is not a miracle. Remember that whether or not I leveraged my purchase of the stock, I would have earned the same amount when I sold it. The difference with leveraging is that I was making money on stocks that I hadn't paid for with my own money, and that is why the profit on my own money was so much higher. I was using other people's money (the bank's, in this case) to make money for myself.

By the same token, had the stock declined I would have lost

money on the shares I had bought with my own money. I would have lost money on the shares I had bought with the bank's money, and also would have lost the interest I had to pay for borrowing it. Leverage is a wonderful tool when the return exceeds the interest paid. But it can sometimes work against you.

How to Make Inflation Work for You

Yet another reason for using other people's money involves inflation. We read in the newspapers that inflation has driven up the rate of interest, and so it has. But it is just as true that inflation makes borrowing profitable, especially over long periods of time. Suppose you earn $30,000 a year and are considering buying a house with a $50,000 mortgage. Your monthly mortgage payments may be $670 or so. This is a big chunk of your current income, I know; but let's look down the road a bit. High levels of inflation may continue. How high? For how long? Let's assume that the inflation rate will rise 10 percent over the next ten years — which is far from impossible. If your income keeps pace with inflation but does not exceed it, at the end of those ten years you will be earning $77,812. But your monthly mortgage installment will still be $670, even after ten years. That $670 now represents a much smaller part of your total income, and the burden it represents is so much the lighter. And, at the same time, you are paying off the loan with dollars that are worth much less than those you borrowed. You are a beneficiary of inflation — one of many, by the way.

Remember, of course, that in the example your income rose only by the amount of inflation. Actually, it will probably rise more than that. Most employers grant cost-of-living increases to their workers. But in addition, employees often receive productivity or merit increases over and above the cost-of-living increase. Furthermore, should you advance in your career, through promotion, by a change of position, or by setting up your own business, you may have unexpected leaps in your earnings. All these will make the loan or future payments even cheaper to you. The main point is simply this: you are paying off long-term, fixed debts with inflated money, so the cost in real dollars is going down; and this is true of any loan whose terms remain fixed.

Most books dealing in financial advice tell you to borrow money for the shortest possible time and to pay it back as quickly as you can. But, as we've just seen, that may not always be the best idea, since you can be paying back the loan in inflated dollars. It is true, of course, that the faster you pay back a loan, the less your actual dollar cost will be. But even that is not as true as it seems to be. For example, a simple loan of $1,000 taken out at 20 percent for one year costs $200. If taken out for two years, the cost is about $400. In this case, paying the loan off in one year saves you the $200 in interest that you would be charged in the second year. But if you take out an installment loan for $1,000 at 20 percent for two years, the actual cost may be far less, because with each installment you are paying back part of the principal, in addition to the interest. You are reducing the amount outstanding on which the interest is being charged.

As you pay off the principal, you have, in effect, less borrowed money to use, and now it is the lender who has the use of the money you have paid back. Using the same example, suppose you borrow $1,000 for two years at 20 percent. After a year, you owe approximately $500. During the first twelve months you have paid back about one-half the principal, $500, and the 20 percent interest, $200. For the coming year, you have only $500 of the borrowed money to use yourself. Twenty percent of $500 is $100, the amount of interest you pay during the second year. After two years, you will have paid $300 in interest, not $400. Most lending institutions charge you interest only on the amount outstanding, so the longer you hold the loan, the less interest you actually pay.

The $10,000 Experiment

Professional economists and statisticians tell us that these are times of "disintermediation." Disintermediation is the flow of money from one source to another as a result of a difference in interest rates. What the economists mean is that more people are moving their money around these days because there is so much competition for money. This competition has created many new opportunities for higher returns. But savings, lending and other financial institutions that handle your money have their hands tied because of strict government regulations. They cannot compete as freely as other types of businesses. Although the Reagan administration is trying to remove restrictive regulations and promote free trade, investors who are not now aware of these opportunities will end up losing them. Let's consider some routes that might be taken by an individual who has saved $10,000, and what can result from borrowing $10,000 and investing it. This should illustrate how much you can lose by not knowing your options and how much you may gain through borrowing.

Savings Accounts

You start out with the $10,000 in a savings account earning 5¾ percent interest compounded daily. That comes to 6 percent if you keep the money in the account for a year. At the end of a year, your bank account will show a balance of $10,600.

Assume that your marginal tax rate on ordinary income is 25 percent. (We discuss marginal tax rates a little further on in the chapter.) You pay $150 in income tax on your earnings, and this leaves you with $10,450. If inflation has been 10 percent during the past year, your $10,000 had to earn $1,000 just to keep up with inflation. So despite your nominal earnings of $450, you have lost $550 of your savings' purchasing power.

Certificates of Deposit

Now let's say that you take the $10,000 out of the savings account and invest it in a CD. The rate of inflation is still 10 percent, and your top-dollar marginal tax rate on ordinary income (including interest and dividends) is 25 percent. But — and here is the difference — the CD pays 16 percent, not 6 percent. At the end of the year you have $11,600, not $10,600. After paying the 25 percent tax, you have $11,200 instead of $10,450. Inflation again has reduced the real profit by $1,000, or 10 percent, down to $10,200 in the values of the previous year. So you have earned, in real terms and after tax, $200 on that initial investment of $10,000, or a 2 percent *real* rate of return. Remember that taxes and inflation are here to stay, so both ought to be taken into account in any calculation.

Borrowing $10,000

Suppose that instead of investing your own $10,000 in a 16 percent CD, you *borrow* $10,000 at 10 percent (for cheap money sources, see Section II) and invest it in the same CD. As before, you end up with nominal earnings of $11,600, and as before you have to pay $400 of that in taxes, so you are left with $11,200. But you paid $1,000 in interest for the use of the initial $10,000, and that interest is fully tax deductible. As a result, your tax bill is $250 lower than it would otherwise have been. So your nominal return is back up to $11,450. Subtracting out the effects of inflation, your real return is $450. You will earn this $450 every year you can continue to borrow at 10 percent and invest at 16 percent. Of course, next year, this $450 will only have the purchasing power of $405 compared to its value this year. But that $450 will be found money, money that you have virtually picked up on the street. This found money will not make you rich, but it will buy you a lot of very nice meals or new clothes, or may even cover your rent or pay your mortgage for a month.

Leveraging

Finally, let's see what would happen if you were to leverage that $10,000 of your own money. In other words, let's say that you use $10,000 to borrow $90,000 at 15 percent a year. The $100,000 buys you x shares of stock. Now, the guiding principle of the investment is your belief that the stock will appreciate at a rate faster than 15 percent, the rate of interest you are paying. Suppose the stock goes up at a compound rate of 20 percent each year. After the first year, the $100,000 is worth $120,000. After deducting $10,125 in interest ($13,500 minus the $3,375 Uncle Sam gives you back), you are left with $9,875. After taxes you will still have $7,406.25. Even assuming that same 10 percent inflation that would reduce the purchasing power of your initial $10,000 investment by $1,000, you still have a return of $6,406.25. This represents an after-tax after-inflation return of over 64 percent on the $10,000 you put in. Not bad for starters. (If the stock goes up!)

Now, assume that you hold on to the stock for ten years. When you sell it, the market value of the stock will be $619,175. You will have paid $135,000 in interest, or perhaps half that if you've been paying back your loan in monthly installments. The pretax profit on your $10,000 is $474,175 ($619,175 minus $135,000 interest minus $10,000 initial investment), or over 4,700 percent on your $10,000 initial investment. *And* your interest is fully tax deductible. Had you invested only your own $10,000 in the same stock, without borrowing anything else, your $10,000 would now be worth $61,917, a pretax gain of $51,917 or about 520 percent.

On the one side: 520 percent. On the other: 4,700 percent. Or $51,917 as opposed to $474,175. That speaks for itself, doesn't it?

Minimizing Taxes

We have mentioned tax liability a few times. Of course there is no one tax rate for each individual. The tax structure is a "graduated" one — meaning that each person's income passes through many tax brackets. The tax on your 10,000th dollar is lower than on your 20,000th dollar. The following table shows the federal tax rates for different income brackets during 1982, 1983 and 1984.

Since state, county and city taxes vary from place to place, we cannot address them here. But don't forget to figure them in yourself.

During 1982, Fred and Margo together earned $50,000. That

Taxable Income Bracket	1982 Tax Rate on Income in Bracket	1983 Tax Rate on Income in Bracket	1984 Tax Rate on Income in Bracket
$0-$3,400	0%	0%	0%
$3,400-$5,500	12	11	11
$5,500-$7,600	14	13	12
$7,600-$11,900	16	15	14
$11,900-$16,000	19	17	16
$16,000-$20,200	22	19	18
$20,200-$24,600	25	23	22
$24,600-$29,900	29	26	25
$29,900-$35,200	33	30	28
$35,200-$45,800	39	35	33
$45,800-$60,000	44	40	38
$60,000-$85,600	49	44	42
$85,600-$109,400	50	48	45
$109,400-$162,400	50	50	49
$162,400-$215,400	50	50	50
$215,400 and over	50	50	50

was their *earned income.* They did not, however, pay taxes on the entire $50,000, because they had many deductions which reduced their gross earned income. These included the standard exemptions for dependents, interest expenses, medical expenses, charitable contributions, child care (nursery school), mortgage payments, etc. In fact, their adjusted gross income was only $35,000.

Fred and Margo also had *unearned income,* which included dividends and interest they received from their investments, and capital gains from price appreciation on stocks they had sold. Their interest and dividends came to $1,200. Since $400 ($200 per person) of their interest and dividends was excluded from taxation, only $800 was taxable at the same rate as their regular income. Fred and Margo also realized a net capital gain of $2,000 on investments they had sold during the year. Since this capital gain was all long term, only $800 of it was taxed, since only 40 percent of capital gains is taxable.

Now let's consider Fred and Margo's tax position as a whole. The two of them had three types of income:

1. Gross earned income	$50,000
2. Gross unearned income	1,200
3. Gross capital gains	2,000
Total gross income	$53,200

But they did not pay taxes on $53,200 — not by a long shot. Their taxable income was as follows:

1. Net adjusted income	$35,000
2. Net unearned income	800
3. Net capital gains	800
Total taxable income	$36,600

$36,600 was the sum on which they paid taxes.

Let's now consider a few of the terms you must understand in order to calculate the taxes on your income and investments — and in order to minimize those taxes!

Taxes Paid

Fred and Margo paid $7,947 in federal taxes for 1982 (the sum of the taxes due for the different income brackets they passed through on their way to $36,600). Their tax payments amounted to 21.7 percent of their taxable income and 15 percent of their gross income. These percentages are not important as such; they simply mean that the Coopers now had $7,947 less than they had earned. They also conceal the fact that you pay different rates on the increments of your earnings.

Top-Dollar Tax Rate

This is the rate at which you are taxed on your top dollars of gross earnings — in other words, the rate you pay on those dollars which are over the lower end of your top tax bracket. For example, Fred and Margo's gross income was $53,200, which put them in the $45,800-to-$60,000 bracket, where the top-dollar tax rate is 44 percent. This means that the $7,400 of their income that falls in this range is taxable at a top-dollar tax rate of 44 percent. This top-dollar tax rate is used to calculate the cost savings associated with deductible expenses, such as interest payments.

Tax-deductible expenses such as interest paid can be deducted from your top dollar of earnings. The net cost to you for such expenditures is significantly reduced, because you are saving the taxes computed at the top-dollar rate that would have been paid on this money had you not used it for tax-deductible purposes. In Fred and Margo's case, a loan of $10,000 at 12 percent interest would have cost them, not $1,200, but $672 — a saving of $528 in taxes that without the deduction they otherwise would have had to pay on $1,200 of their earnings at 44 percent.

Marginal Tax Rate

The marginal tax rate is the rate at which you are taxed on amounts earned over and above your current total taxable income. This rate is particularly important when you expect a high return on your investments. Such returns can add significant amounts to your income, which will make the tax bite much bigger. Fred and Margo would have had to pay a 39 percent federal tax on any additional taxable income above $36,600 and below $45,800. That 39 percent is their *marginal tax rate.* If their incremental investment return had exceeded $9,000, the excess over $9,000 would have been taxed at 44 percent, the rate in the next tax bracket.

But don't despair. The new maximum federal tax has been lowered from 70 percent to 50 percent, and the maximum capital gains tax is now 20 percent. (To explain, only 40 percent of capital gains is taxable, and 40 percent of 50 percent equals 20 percent.) Marginal tax rates should be used in calculating the tax consequences of making incremental returns on your investments. There may be factors that make it difficult to project your earnings — bonuses or commissions, perhaps a promotion. Your investment returns cannot be determined because of interest rate changes, price fluctuations, etc. In such cases, use your best estimate.

And finally, even though paying taxes is painful, wouldn't you rather be paying them on large amounts of money than not have the money on which to pay taxes? After all, you do get to keep a big portion for yourself.

Risk — What Is It?

Every time you make an investment, you confront three different kinds of risk. The first is the possibility that the return on your investment will have less real value as time goes on, so that you will have less and less real purchasing power. In plain English, this kind of risk is called inflation. The second kind of risk is loss of principal, the possibility that the investment itself will be worth less in nominal terms, as when a stock's price goes down. The third kind, *opportunity cost,* is more complex. Whenever you make an investment, the money you have used is no longer available to be used in some other way. For example, when I used $2,000 of my own money to buy $20,000 worth of stock, I lost the use of that $2,000 and whatever return might have been made from it. Opportunity cost is money you could have made but did not, for one of several reasons.

Let's look at these three kinds of risk in greater detail.

Inflation

We have seen that when you invest your money in a savings account at 5¾ percent interest, you are really losing money, because even a 6 percent rate of return is lower than the current rate of inflation. What you want is a "cushion," the difference between your after-tax return on any investment and the current rate of inflation. That cushion is your real rate of return on your investment.

Sometimes a cushion is merely temporary. For example, you buy a stock at a certain price, in a year when it is paying a certain dividend. In the next year the dividend may change, the price may change and inflation may change, too. And so too will your real rate of return and thus your cushion. If the return falls low enough, you may not have a cushion at all. But when you put your money into what is called a *fixed-income investment,* you can try to "lock in" that cushion for a number of years. In a fixed-income investment — such as treasury bills, treasury bonds, treasury notes, CDs, corporate bonds, tax-exempt bonds, and convertible bonds — the amount of interest you will get for each bond is fixed up to the point when the investment matures. When you buy the bond at a stated price you know exactly what your yield is going to be: the amount the bond pays annually divided by the amount you paid for it. You can lock in such a yield for a year — or for five, ten, twenty, or even thirty years. The problem is that you cannot lock in the rate of inflation. If inflation goes down, you are the winner, because your real rate of return (the after-tax yield minus inflation) will be that much higher; but if inflation goes up, your cushion will shrink and may even be eliminated. That's why future inflation and future interest rates are so critical to the success of fixed-income strategies.

Loss of Principal

So far, we have been talking about the real (after-inflation) value of the *return* on an investment. But what about the value of the investment itself? That too can rise or fall. You know from reading the newspapers that in a "bull market" or "up market" the price of stocks goes up, and in a "bear market" or "down market" the price generally goes down. That is what I mean by loss (and gain) of principal.

The risk of losing your principal in the long run is almost zero when you buy an "illiquid" fixed-income instrument — one that cannot be sold by its purchaser — such as a CD. You won't lose money because you cannot panic and sell it, and when it comes due you will get back the principal plus the interest. But if you invest in a bond of long-term maturity, the price may fluctuate over time, although the interest payment to you will remain the same. The re-sale value of bonds reacts conversely to long-term interest rates.

When interest rates rise, the value of the bonds falls; when long-term interest rates drop, the value of the bonds rises.

As for stocks, their value sometimes fluctuates in response to anticipated future economic conditions — such factors as a change in interest rates on other investments, future inflation, and projections of future levels of corporate profits. But often a stock's value will move up or down because of something that is specific to the company that issued it. For example, if a company announces a new product that seems likely to do very well, investors may buy that company's stock in the belief that the company's profits, and therefore future dividends, will rise. They might buy it even if they felt that the prospects of the economy as a whole were not bright.

Remember, the stock market is an "auction" market. When the people who want to buy a stock outnumber those who want to sell it, the price goes up. When more people want to sell it than buy it, the price goes down.

Opportunity Cost

The risk of buying a stock at, say, $10, and then watching its value fall to $5 is easy to understand. Most of us have also personally experienced the way inflation undermines the return we get on such investments as bank accounts. But risk in the form of opportunity cost is a mystery to most of us. In the business world, opportunity cost is money that could have been made but was not.

There are four kinds of opportunity costs. The first is simply an unused opportunity to get the maximum return on your own assets, with no additional risk. Say you have $10,000 invested in a savings account earning 6 percent a year. This money could have been invested in a certificate of deposit earning 16 percent. By leaving the money in a savings account, you are throwing an extra 10 percent a year out the window.

The second kind of opportunity cost is the failure to use outside money that is available to you. People in varied circumstances have different sources of unused funds, but the most common are profit-sharing funds, life insurance policies, and credit union plans, all of which may provide low-cost loans. Many people can borrow from these sources at 12 percent or even less, and then invest that money at 16 percent. At first glance the opportunity cost to the individual who neglects to make such a loan appears to be 4 percent, but it is really a bit higher, because the interest on the loan is tax deductible.

Among other sources of money that many people overlook are the many foundations and universities, corporations, states and government agencies that offer grants, scholarships, and loans. (See Section II for sources of money.)

Finally, there are some who label as an opportunity cost the failure to take advantage of an investment opportunity or failure to play such an opportunity to its fullest advantage. Take an investor who buys 1,000 shares of stock at $10 each, or $10,000 in all. The price of the stock goes up to $15 a share, so the investor sells, making a profit of $5,000. Shortly afterward, the stock goes up again . . . to $20 a share. The investor might have made a $10,000 profit instead of $5,000. The opportunity cost was therefore $5,000.

This last kind of opportunity cost is too elusive for us to worry about. At any given moment, there are literally millions of investment opportunities that one might be able to afford. Let's say there are five million of them, with an average return of $1,000 each. It is really pointless to say that all of us are missing the optimum opportunity. You know that 16 percent from a CD is a better return than 6 percent from a savings account; but no one, however shrewd or well informed, can accurately predict the highs and lows of the stock market as a whole, let alone an individual stock. An investor who takes profits in line with his investment goals has acted wisely no matter how much extra money he might have made by holding out a little longer.

This last kind of opportunity cost does serve one purpose: the investor has a good story to tell at cocktail parties. "Let me tell you what I could have earned" tales make interesting conversation. This book, however, deals with more substantial information, so we shall be looking only at the more real kinds of opportunity costs — more real because you can actually do something about them.

Calculating Your Risk Tolerance

Personal Risk Tolerance

For each of us, there is a limit to the amount of risk we can tolerate. And that limit is as uniquely personal as our fingerprints. Oftentimes the ability to tolerate risk has nothing whatever to do with our income or our assets, but everything to do with our background and our personalities. People who remember the Great Depression, people who worry about their assets, people who want to see, feel, and smell their money — all have a low tolerance for risk. These individuals tense up with every fluctuation in prices. Let the value of their investments drop ever so slightly and they begin to bite their nails. Let the value of their investments go up, and they continue to bite their nails: "Whatever goes up," they reason, "must come down." They can relax only when their investments are sold or liquidated. These people should not invite so much risk as those who would not lose a wink.

Your emotional (as opposed to financial) ability to bear risk is your *personal risk tolerance.*

To determine your own personal risk tolerance, take the following quiz, by marking the answers that best describe you:

1. Would I worry if my investment went down in price by:

    a. 10 percent _____?

    b. 25 percent _____?

    c. 50 percent _____?

2. Would I sell my investment if it went up by:

    a. 10 percent _____?

    b. 50 percent _____?

    c. 100 percent _____?

3. Would I lose sleep if my money were not insured by the government?

   a. Yes   _____.

   b. Maybe   _____.

   c. No   _____.

4. I enjoy reading the financial section of the newspaper.

   a. Never   _____.

   b. Sometimes _____.

   c. Always   _____.

5. I can make investment decisions on my own.

   a. Never   _____.

   b. Sometimes _____.

   c. Always   _____.

6. Every time interest rates change, I

   a. Become apprehensive   _____.

   b. Wait to see what will happen   _____.

   c. Look for new investment opportunities _____.

Now, give yourself 1 point for each "a" answer, 2 points for each "b" answer, and 3 points for each "c" answer.

If your score is 6, you have no risk tolerance. Stick to the cost-savings and no-risk strategies.

If your score is between 7 and 9, you have a low risk tolerance. To avoid losing sleep, stick mostly to cost savings, no-risk and low-risk strategies.

If your score is between 10 and 13, you have an average degree of risk tolerance. You should invest in high-risk strategies only if you have set aside "play money": cash to invest (and possibly lose) that is over and above what you will need to fulfill expenses.

If your score is 14 to 18 you are a gambler, and you are emotionally well suited to invest in leveraged or high-risk investments.

Financial Risk Tolerance

Now that you know your personal risk tolerance, let's calculate your financial risk tolerance — your financial ability to sustain financial losses. Before you can make this calculation, you must know how much you earn and how much you spend. To learn this, it will be helpful to fill out the worksheets following.

GOAL WORKSHEET — CURRENT AND ONGOING EXPENSES

	Current Estimated Monthly Expenses	Estimated Monthly Expenses One Year from Now	Estimated Monthly Expenses Ten Years from Now
1. Food and beverages			
2. Shelter			
3. Clothing			
4. Protection against risk (insurance):			
life insurance			
homeowners insurance			
car insurance			
5. Entertainment			
6. Education			
7. Medical and health care costs			
8. Transportation			
9. "Rainy day" fund			
10. Cost of credit			
11. Travel and recreation			

12. Personal business matters _____ _____ _____

13. Miscellaneous personal _____ _____ _____

14. "Luxuries" _____ _____ _____

15. Charity and religious expenses _____ _____ _____

16. Income taxes _____ _____ _____

MAJOR FUTURE GOALS

	How Much Will Be Needed	When It Will Be Needed	Amount per Year
Education	_____	_____	_____
Housing (new shelter)	_____	_____	_____
Retirement	_____	_____	_____
"Stake" for your children	_____	_____	_____
"Stake" for yourself	_____	_____	_____
Care of elderly or disabled	_____	_____	_____
"One-shot" expenses	_____	_____	_____
Major "rainy day" fund	_____	_____	_____

Filling in this chart will help you to calculate your current budget as well as to evaluate your future needs. Calculating your budget as a percent of your earnings will help you to determine what is left over for investments or savings.

Sure, inflation will increase the dollar amount of your spending, but it will also increase your earnings.

Now answer the following questions to determine your financial risk tolerance:

1. If I lose the money I've invested, can I replace it? The answer depends on how much you are earning, how much you need in order to live the way you want to, and how much you can save. If you save $5,000 a year, you can lose $5,000 and replace it in one year. Of course nobody wants or plans to lose $5,000; that figure simply represents the maximum limit of your financial ability to make up losses.

2. If I lose the money I've invested, will my life-style change? To find the answer, ask a few more questions: Do I depend on my savings to supplement my income? Is my income higher than my expenses? Do I have additional potential sources of income?

If your expenses are higher than your income and you depend on other sources such as a pension, social security, or earnings on your investments to make up the difference, your financial risk tolerance is quite low. You should be looking only at cost-saving, no-risk, and low-risk strategies.

3. What rate of return do I expect from my investments? If you are relying on your assets to produce or supplement your income, make sure they earn enough for your purposes by finding out just how much in such earnings you do need. Let's say that you find you need at least $15,000 a year. If you have $200,000 in all to invest, you could use $100,000 to buy 15 percent intermediate bonds (maturing in one to seven years). This will guarantee your $15,000, and you can invest the other $100,000 in inflation hedges or in riskier securities. Of course, if you need $30,000, you will want to lock in that 15 percent yield on your entire savings.

You now know whether you are a high-risk, a medium-risk, a low-risk, or a no-risk personality. You also know your tolerance for financial risk. You can use this knowledge of your character and your financial situation to form a game plan. But remember that no one should gamble with every penny; even high-risk types should invest only a part of their assets in high-risk investments; the rest of their money should be placed with greater caution.

Degrees of Risk

The basic axiom of investing is simply this: the higher the potential risk, the greater the potential rewards. The potential risk in most high-risk investments is the loss of your principal; the potential reward is a high return on your investment. However, low risk doesn't necessarily imply a low reward — particularly at times like the present, when interest rates are very high and competition for money is very strong. Let's take a look at the kinds of investments best suited to the various degrees of risk tolerance.

No Risk
The no-risk category includes all-saver certificates, treasury bills (three months to one year), and short-term CDs (six months to one year). These investments do carry minimal risks, but mostly in the opportunity cost area. In other words, when you invest in a liquid or very short term asset, you choose security over the chance to lock in a high return in interest in the face of a general decline in rates.

Liquid Reserves (or Money Market Funds). You will need to have immediate access to part of your funds so that you can pay your bills and make occasional large purchases such as a car or a television set. These funds offer you not only immediate access to your money but also fairly high rates of interest, in contrast to checking accounts, which usually pay you little or no interest at all.

Low Risk
This category includes short-term bonds, treasury notes (one to five years), intermediate bonds of one to five years, long-term CDs

(more than one year), and convertible stocks (which, unlike common stocks, have a fixed dividend and a prior claim on corporate assets). The common denominators in all these investments are low risk of principal loss but the potential for opportunity cost.

Medium Risk

Stocks and long-term bonds can also fit into this category. Although stocks are really high-risk investments, use of the strategies in Section IV helps to limit the downside risk and capitalize the upside profits. Many people regard common stocks as an inflation hedge; and, indeed, if we look at the past 75 years, they have been. But stocks are still fairly volatile in the short run and can serve as an inflation hedge only if held in a diversified portfolio over long periods of time, such as five years, ten years, or complete market cycles.

Inflation Hedges

These include such tangibles as real estate, art, precious stones, currencies, gold and other precious metals; and collectibles such as antiques, stamps and rare coins. During times of inflation these tend to become objects of intense speculation and therefore their value increases. Should we enter a period of "stagflation," when inflation goes down and stays there, or a period of deflation, these investments lose value.

High Risk

High risk means that you can "go for broke." You stand the chance of making a bundle. But you also face the possibility of losing your shirt. Perhaps a bit more too.

Actually, there is nothing wrong with high-risk investments. We make them all the time. If you ever bought a lottery ticket or a chance on a raffle, you made a high-risk investment. You did not get your initial investment back after the drawing. To make high-risk investments, you need to remember that risk means just that — risk. To be comfortable with it, you need a high level of risk tolerance. You also need to know exactly what you are putting at stake.

Minimal Risk

Savings Accounts

What could be safer than a savings account? The bank looks after your money, the Federal Deposit Insurance Corporation (FDIC) insures it against loss, and it is yours on demand. Best of all, your money earns interest, an average rate of 6 percent. In one sense, a savings account is a safe investment; you are not likely ever to lose your principal. The risk lies in the fact that your earnings will not keep pace with the rate of inflation, so that in real terms you are losing money. And you also suffer an opportunity cost, for many other safe investments earn a good deal more than 6 percent interest.

Many people keep their money in savings banks simply for the peace of mind it affords. This peace of mind is in part an illusion, for the FDIC and other federal insurance facilities insure only your principal, not the interest you have earned on it. Should your savings bank fail, you could lose that interest — insignificant though it may seem. Besides, the FDIC will only insure an account up to $100,000. To circumvent this, when your original account approaches the ceiling of $100,000, you have to open a new account in another bank. Or, if you want to stay with the same bank, you must open a new account in another name, for example, one in the name of your spouse, a joint account, or a trust account for a child.

Money Market Funds

Still, when all is said and done, savings accounts are unquestionably safe; at least you will never lose your principal. Even so, people who keep their money in savings banks solely for safety's sake are still suffering from an illusion — the idea that only savings banks are safe — because there are other safe *and* convenient depositories for your money. Take money market funds, for example. Your investment in such a fund is as safe as the under-lying "instruments" (or investments) that make it up. And almost all of these investments — treasury bills, certificates of deposit, commercial paper, bankers' acceptances, and Eurodollar certif-icates — are very, very safe indeed. The reason is that all of them have short maturities, ranging from one week to one year. These short-term notes have to be paid ahead of all other debts, and the interest the funds receive on them is very closely tied to the rate of inflation. As a result, the funds' principal is safe, and their earn-ings are high enough to allow them to pay interest to their depositors at rates that produce pretax earnings equal to, and generally higher than, the level of inflation. Thus the risk of re-duced purchasing power is minimal, and the risk of losing your principal is virtually zero. So where is the risk? Simply this: the in-terest the funds pay their depositors fluctuates. The rates do go up and down. On the other hand, money market funds are highly "liquid"; in other words, you can withdraw your money whenever you want to. Many such funds give you so-called debit cards or checks; most will even provide wire transfers for amounts over $500. In many cases it is easier to get your money from a money market fund than to get it from your checking account at the bank.

All-Savers Certificates

All-savers are as safe as the assets behind the company or bank that issues them — and that usually means they are safe indeed. An exception may be some of the small savings banks and savings and loan cooperatives that are having serious financial problems in part because so many of their depositors have closed their 6 per-cent accounts to invest their money elsewhere at higher rates. For-tunately, however, a recent regulation removed the interest-rate ceilings on some types of certificates issued by thrift institutions, so they can now offer more competitive terms.

The risks in an all-savers come mostly in the form of op-portunity costs, for in order to get the high rate of interest, you have to lock in your money for a year. If you should need it during that period, you will find getting access to it quite costly. (For more information on all-savers, see Section III: Investment Vehicles Explained.)

Certificates of Deposit (CDs)

Certificates of deposit are insured by the FDIC (Federal Deposit Insurance Corporation) or the FSLIC (Federal Savings & Loan Insurance Corporation); but, as with savings accounts, only the principal is insured, and that only up to $100,000. Like the all-savers, CDs are time deposits, however, and their interest is fully taxable. They may be purchased for periods of six months to four years. Withdrawing the money before the "due date" will subject you to heavy penalties. On the other hand, CDs offer much higher returns than regular day-of-deposit/day-of-withdrawal savings accounts. The current strong competition has forced many banks to offer investments that combine high interest rates with greater liquidity, or investments that require less than the $10,000 minimum usual for CDs. But if you cannot avail yourself of these advantages for your CD, you may have an opportunity cost.

Unlike money market funds, whose interest rates change daily, CDs are fixed-interest investments, and that is both an advantage and a disadvantage. If interest rates go up after you have bought your CD, you are the loser; you suffer an opportunity cost. However, interest rates may go down as well as up. You might buy a six-month CD paying 15 percent in June and then watch interest rates fall to 10 percent in July. You would still get the 15 percent for an additional five months.

Treasury Bills

Among the devices the government uses to finance its legendary deficits are treasury bills. Some people think these are just about the safest investments around; after all, they are backed by the full faith and credit and assets of the U.S. government. Others feel that for these very reasons, treasury bills would get a poor rating if the government's financial health were ever to be evaluated by the means used for public corporations. And they may well be right. *Business Week* recently reported that between 1974 and 1980 the interest on the public debt rose by almost 270 percent, from $20.3 billion to $74.9 billion. When this article appeared, Uncle Sam was paying 12.5 percent interest on borrowed money; but in 1981 the cost of the debt was much higher, about 15.5 percent on average, or 20 percent of all federal spending. This is not the total debt outstanding, by the way, but only the *debt service* on the total debt outstanding. What successful business pays out 20 percent of its revenues in debt service?

What would happen if the yardsticks used by securities analysts to evaluate corporate issues were applied to the U.S. government? In 1979, General Motors, with sales of more than $67 billion, paid out just $400 million in interest on all its debts, including dividends on preferred stock. In other words, every dollar of interest owed by GM was covered by more than $167 in annual sales. But if we examine the figures for the federal government, we find that in fiscal 1979 each dollar of interest paid by the U.S. was covered by only about $6 in tax receipts. Of course, General Motors doesn't have taxing authority. But this is still an interesting point to think about, now that the national debt stands at the $1 trillion (a thousand billion dollars) level. Even so, the government is not likely to default on short-term debts such as treasury bills, or on long-term bonds either, for that matter. Your true risk comes in the form of opportunity risk, not default, since treasury bills are not very liquid. If our government should ever be unable to pay off its short-term debts, the reason will be that our whole financial system has fallen apart. In that case, you will probably have more important things to worry about than the treasury bills you may own. Until that day of Armageddon, t-bills will no doubt go on paying rates of interest closely linked to inflation, so they give you a good chance of keeping up with it.

Medium Risk

Bonds

You may recall that in explaining why money market funds are quite safe, I pointed out that most of their money is invested in short-term debt instruments (such as A1P1 commercial paper, t-bills, CDs, etc.). These are among the safest kind of debt instruments. Intermediate-term bonds, either corporate, government, state or municipal, are also a kind of debt. They are somewhat more risky; still, the risk is slight. Moody's Investors Service and Standard & Poor's rate all bonds for safety and soundness, so that the mystery is largely eliminated. The ratings go from AAA, the highest; to AA, very high but somewhat less so; down through A, Baa, Ba, B, and bbb. Stick with AAA, AA, and A bonds, for the most part, though the higher interest that lower-rated bonds are forced to offer may sometimes seem to justify the additional risk of a Baa bond.

The real risk in buying a bond is not so much default as the fluctuation of bond prices. As interest rates go up, the value of a bond goes down; as interest rates go down, a bond's value goes up. If the bond's value does go up, you can sell it and make a capital gain. You can also make a capital gain if you buy the bond below its face value of, say, $1,000 and then hold it to maturity, when you will get the full $1,000 from the company that issued it. Moreover, when bond prices are low, the yields of bonds are high, because bonds are fixed-income investments, and the lower the price, the higher the rate of return.

High Risk

Common Stocks — A "Tame" Risk

Common stocks may be a medium or high risk investment. They are riskier investments than bank accounts and money market funds because they give you no protection for your principal. They are also riskier than bonds because they are not fixed-income investments and give you no protection for your return; the dividends may fluctuate. There are, nonetheless, a number of strategies for making money on stocks.

Let's say your broker tells you about a company that has been losing money steadily. It has been laying off workers; it is overstocked with inventory; things are a mess. Why is he enthusiastic about this stock? Because he figures that it has gone about as low as it can go, and that its price will soon move up. But then again, maybe it won't; maybe the company will continue operating, with declining earnings and rising inventories, or maybe it will go bankrupt.

In the case of bankruptcy, the company may file for Chapter XI and continue to operate under the control and guidance of outside agencies. As a common stockholder you can claim your share of the assets of the company only after Uncle Sam and a lot of others. Any outstanding taxes must be paid first. Pension fund participants are next in queue. Creditors and bondholders are next. If these prior claims exceed the liquidation value of the company — what is realized from the conversion of all assets to cash — you as a common stockholder get nothing.

Fortunately, this grim picture is rare. In this country over 8,600 stocks are publicly traded. In fewer than one-tenth of one percent of bankruptcies does the common stockholder end up with nothing. The common experience is to get back at least 50 cents on each dollar invested. Occasionally you can even make money. When Penn Central filed Chapter XI, some hardy types held on to their stock. Because of subsequent appreciations, they got their money back. And those who were willing to buy the stock when it hit bottom made as much as twenty times their investment.

Suppose that *all* stocks are doing badly. Your broker may tell you that the market is loaded with bargains; that interest rates are going to go down next week, next month, or next year; and that any stock you buy now will be worth twice as much in twelve months' time. Maybe. But maybe it will take more than twelve months to correct the conditions that have driven stock prices down to their present low levels.

Say a stock sells for $12 and earns $4 a share. Its "price-to-earn-ings" (P/E) ratio is then 3. That means that you have to put up $3 to get $1 of earnings; in all, a pretty low ratio. This may indeed be a bargain. But sometimes the price of the stock is low for a good reason — for example, because the market believes that a company's current earnings will not continue to increase in the future and may even go down. In that case, the stock's price will probably remain low; or it might go even lower, in which case you would have a capital loss if and when you decided to sell the stock.

Some brokers, by the way, suggest almost the opposite strategy: buying stocks with high P/Es on the theory that their prices or earnings will rise even further.

All these ways of making money through stocks can also be ways of losing it. Common stocks are a risky investment, and they should be considered only by people with a tolerance for risk. But the risks of such investments can be controlled. The main point is to know when to cut your losses and when to take your profits. If a stock is going down in value, don't wait for months as it keeps go-ing down and down, hoping that at last it will pick up.

Example: You buy 100 shares of ABC stock at $10 each. The stock begins to drop — $9, $8, $7 — all the way down to $5 a share. At this point you sell. You have lost $500. Yet keep in mind that you could have reduced your losses by selling the stock when it hit $9, or $8, or $7. You could have controlled your loss. Per-haps the stock bottomed out at $5 and then began to climb back — to $10, and then higher, to $11, $12, or whatever. Should you have been willing to risk it and hold on to that stock?

Common stock, therefore, might be called a rather tame risky investment. Those with a high risk tolerance can put their money in really chancy instruments such as options, commodities, and financial futures.

Some investments may cost you not only every cent you've put in but also more. You will recall our discussion of leveraged invest-ments. That story had a happy ending. But not all such stories do. Suppose you buy 100 shares of stock at $10 a share, putting down

$100 and borrowing $900. Ninety percent of the purchase is lever-aged. The stock then goes down to $5 a share, and you decide to cut your losses and sell. You have lost all of what you invested plus $400 plus the interest on the borrowed portion besides. Remember that almost anything that creates the possibility of great gains also creates the possibility of great losses.

Still, high-risk investments can be exciting, and you can use them and still limit your losses.

Play-Money Strategy

Anyone under sixty who has more than $1,000 in liquid assets should have some "play money" — money to use for the sheer fun of adventure and the potential for "making it big." The only excep-tions here are the no-risk personalities. The sum can be $500, $1,000, or any suitable amount (limited to 50 percent of your net worth), and it should be invested in such a way that the most you can lose is the sum you have invested. Suitable investments for this money include options and lotteries, and stock in small, emerging growth companies. Some of these strategies may have a higher downside risk than others — leveraging, for example — but we will learn how to control that risk in Section IV.

Setting aside "play money" can limit your risk when you are dabbling in high-risk investments.

The following strategy increases your probability of winning. First divide your play money into five equal parts. Invest only a fifth of it at any one time and leave the remaining four-fifths in a money market fund or other low- or no-risk investments. If your initial investment succeeds, start plowing back a part of your profit into high-risk investments, but put your original one-fifth investment back into the money market fund. Do this every time you make a profit. If you really strike it rich, you may want to stop making high-risk investments. Otherwise, put aside a portion of your profits and continue to play with the rest. This cuts somewhat into your ability to "make a bundle," but it will help to ensure that you will end up ahead in the long run. Should the first investment result in a loss, you still have four more times "at bat." If you find you have "struck out" the first three times at bat, reexamine your source of information and the timing of the strategy.

Finding Your Net Worth

Before you know how much money you can invest, you need to know your net worth.

In order to simplify the process of calculating your net worth, you may want to use the following forms to determine your current investment profile and the total value of your investable assets.

On your personal financial statement, use current values wherever available. When they are not available, "guesstimate."

Remember, the bottom line, *net worth,* is not the last word, because you can increase your net worth in three ways:

1. By reducing your liabilities,
2. By adding to your assets, or
3. By increasing the value of your present assets.

To reduce your liabilities, you can cut down on your expenses, and you can pay off part of your debts or reduce the cost of carrying them. Any money you save in these or any other ways increases your assets. You can add to your assets by putting a portion of your income aside regularly for investments rather than spending it. And you can increase the value of those assets by getting your money to work harder for you by investing it more wisely.

Your Investment Game Plan

Now that you know your net worth and your financial and emotional ability to tolerate risk, you can work out your own game plan. Let's consider three separate examples:

WORKSHEET
PERSONAL FINANCIAL STATEMENT

Assets		Liabilities	
Current		Current accounts payable	
Cash in banks		Loans	_____
Checking	_____	Bills	_____
Savings	_____		
Cash reserves		Taxes	_____
T-bills & CDs	_____	Other	_____
Money market funds	_____	Long-Term	
Stocks	_____	Mortgages payable	_____
Bonds	_____	Other debts	_____
Receivables (money owed to you)	_____	Other	_____
		TOTAL LIABILITIES	_____
Long-term			
Real estate			
Residence	_____		
Rental and other properties	_____		
Personal property			
Jewelry	_____		
Furs	_____		
Other properties	_____		
Cash value life insurance	_____		
Collectibles (coins, stamps, antiques)	_____		
Other assets (e.g., profit-sharing or pension funds, IRAs or Keoghs)	_____	Total assets	_____
		Total liabilities	−_____
TOTAL ASSETS	_____	NET WORTH	=_____

YOUR CURRENT INVESTMENT PROFILE

STOCKS Name	Number of Shares	Current Price*	Value (price × shares)
Example: XYZ Company	1000	$6½	$6,500
		TOTAL $	

FIXED INCOME (bonds, liquid reserves, etc.)	Number of Bonds	Current Price*	Value (price × number of bonds)
Example: ABC 16's 91	5	$95	$4,750
		TOTAL $	

*To arrive at true price, multiply quoted price by 10.

1. No risk

Retired people might divide their assets in the following way: play money:

Liquid reserves	15%
Low risk	45%
Inflation hedges	20%
Medium risk	20%
"Play money"	0%

2. Low-to-medium risk

The game plan of a couple in their forties with two children approaching college age might look like this:

Liquid reserves	5%
Low risk	15%
Inflation hedges	40%
Medium risk	30%
"Play money"	10%

3. Medium-to-high risk

A young couple might divide their income as follows:

Liquid reserves	10%
Low risk	0%
Inflation hedges	30%
Medium risk	45%
"Play money"	15%

4. High risk

A single person with no obligations or dependents may have the following game plan:

Liquid reserves	20%
Low risk	0%
Medium risk	0%
Inflation hedges	30%
High risk and "play money"	50%

You will note that in all three cases a significant percentage has been sunk in inflation hedges. I am assuming that many of these households own a home, and that they are not collectors of Ming porcelain. Sometimes, by the way, real estate can produce very high income, as with rental properties. If you own such assets, you may want to put more money into the medium-risk category.

YOUR INVESTMENT GAME PLAN

(1) Risk Category	(2) Percent of Investable Net Worth	(3) Dollar Amounts	(4) Expected Rate of Return
Liquid reserves	_____	_____	_____
Low risk	_____	_____	_____
Medium risk	_____	_____	_____
Inflation hedges	_____	_____	_____
High risk & "play money"	_____	_____	_____

Column (1): The risk categories.
    (2): Percent of investable net worth: investable net worth is that portion of your net worth that is available to you to be invested. Receivables don't count.
    (3): Helps you to translate the percentage into dollars so that you can plainly see what amounts you are working with.
    (4): Encourages you to try to forecast future returns. Of course, if your anticipated return on a higher-risk category is lower than the expected return on a lower-risk category, you should give serious thought to transferring some of your assets into that high-return, lower-risk category.

Changing Your Game Plan

Don't become tied to your game plan. It is meant to be a guide, not a hindrance. In the first place, your circumstances may change: you may come into a large inheritance or win a lottery. Of course, if you win $1 million in a lottery, you will not go out and purchase a million $1 lottery tickets. As your needs and circumstances change, so should your game plan.

It may also make sense at times to reallocate your assets among the risk categories. For example, there are times when it seems wise to put all of your intermediate-risk (or other) investments into a money market fund. When? In my view, just after a big stock market runup, when everything looks just rosy. Yet that is when most investment professionals are particularly euphoric about the market's future. I disagree, because it is hard to predict the course of the market, and your hope that prices will continue to rise may be doomed to disappointment. How, after all, do you know when things are rosy? When you read it in the newspapers. The columnists reflect the views of investment professionals, who are often misleading and sometimes contradictory. Prices are high at the end of a bull market, when investment professionals tend to be most euphoric, and low in a bear market. To me, it makes more sense to buy when the world seems to be coming to an end — toward the end of a bear market — and to sell toward the end of a bull market. How long do you have to wait for the suitable moment to buy or sell stocks? Historically, bear markets have been short in duration; they last about a year or two. Bull markets tend to build up gradually and usually last from three to five years.

After making his millions in the market, J. P. Morgan said that the only thing he knew for sure was that the market would go up and down. None of us knows for sure when the market's turning points will come, but we can all benefit from studying the history of the market.

SECTION II
SOURCES
OF MONEY

Y ou can get your hands on two kinds of money. The first kind comprises your own money, the money you can borrow against your own money, and the money that other people owe you. The second kind is other people's money. This second kind of money source — borrowing, to use another term for it — is the only one that most people know about. Borrowing is a common way of raising cash, and a useful one. But it is more expensive to borrow other people's money than to use your own. However, "your own" money includes the money you can borrow *against* your money — the money in your bank account, for example, or in a life insurance policy or a profit-sharing account; and such loans are far cheaper than ordinary ones.

Many of us have far more money to borrow against than we know about. So let's start by looking at the cheapest kind of money: your own.

Your Own Money

The money you already have is by far the easiest to get hold of, besides being the cheapest. All you really have to do is identify potential sources and then claim what is yours. You don't have to demonstrate your financial stability, your earning power, or your creditworthiness, since the money you are getting hold of is your own. In most cases, it's just a matter of filling out a form requesting the money, then waiting for someone to give it to you.

Bank Accounts

You already know that the money you've deposited at the bank is yours. But you may not know all the ways you can use that money, for most of us only think about spending our money or investing it. But there's a third choice, too. Suppose you have a debt of $1,000 at 24 percent interest. That's $240 interest a year. Let's also say that you have $1,000 in a savings account. If you could earn more than 24 percent interest on your own money at the bank, it would make sense to leave your money there and use it to pay off the interest on your debt, keeping the difference for yourself. (Of course, you would have to pay off the loan itself with money from some other source.) But since you can't earn 24 percent interest on a bank account, or even on a money market account, it makes sense to pay off the loan; thus you will at least save the difference between the 24 percent interest you were paying for your loan and whatever interest you were getting for the money in your bank account.

There's another way of using the cash in your bank account, too, though it requires you to borrow: you can take out a loan from the bank where that money is deposited, using your bankbook as collateral, or security. (If you don't repay any part of the loan, the bank can take the difference from your account.) When you borrow against the money in your bank account, you generally pay lower rates of interest than for any other kind of loan. And your money stays in the bank and continues to earn interest, which you can use to help pay the interest on your loan. You can't withdraw your money until the loan is paid off, but in the end you have borrowed the money at about 1 percent interest a year. That's almost free money. Of course this assumes that the money was put into a certificate of deposit rather than a 5¾ or 6 percent savings account.

Since you cannot use your passbook until the loan is paid off anyway, it's best to put the money in a certificate of deposit. The interest you earn on a CD is much higher than that paid on a day-of-deposit/day-of-withdrawal account. Right now you can earn over 16 percent interest a year on a certificate of deposit, and most banks insure CDs up to $100,000 per account, precisely as they insure a regular savings account.

Life Insurance

Just as you can borrow against the money in your bank account, you can borrow money against the *cash value* of your whole-life insurance policy. This cash value is the amount (which increases over time) that the life insurance company would refund to you at any given time if you decided to terminate the policy. Mind you, by borrowing against the cash value you *do not* terminate the policy.

It's important, of course, to put the money into investments that will earn a higher rate of interest than you are paying for the loan, so you'll be able to pay off the interest and keep the difference for yourself. This isn't hard, since in most cases the interest on the loan won't be very high. Depending on the state you live in and the original date on which you took out the life insurance policy, you can borrow the cash value for as little as 5 to 8 percent interest per year. But it's also important to put the money into a safe investment; remember that if any part of the loan isn't repaid, the insurance company will deduct the unpaid portion from the policy's *face value,* the amount your beneficiary will get when you die. If your investments are safe, your heirs will inherit them as well, on top of your policy's face value.

There's another feature to this kind of loan, too, besides the low interest rates. In most cases, you don't have to pay the interest outright; instead, you can have the life insurance company deduct it from your future cash value as it is accrued. What happens in this case, however, is that you end up paying interest on not only the original loan but also the interest charges that are added to it. Therefore using this feature will increase your cost of borrowing.

Say, for example, that you take out a loan of $1,000 at 8 percent interest for five years. At the end of the first year, you will be paying interest on $1,080 ($1,000 + [$1,000 x 0.08]), and at the end of the second year you will be paying interest on $1,166.40 ($1,080 + [$1,080 x 0.08]). In fact, at the end of the five years, the actual interest rate will be 9.4 percent, not 8 percent.

There is another very good reason to pay the interest rather than having it deducted from your policy's cash value. Since all interest payments are fully tax deductible, paying the interest *each year* further reduces your cost of borrowing by the amount of your marginal tax rate. For example, a taxpayer in the 50 percent marginal tax bracket who is paying 8 percent interest will get half of that money back from Uncle Sam at the end of the year.

The regulations that cover borrowing against life insurance policies vary from state to state, but in most places you can borrow the full cash value at very low rates of interest. Several states have passed laws that allow life insurance companies to charge competitive — that is, much higher — interest rates on money borrowed against policies now being initiated or purchased recently. But if you've had your policy for longer than a year or two, you can still borrow at the much lower old rates.

Profit-Sharing Plans

Another fund you can borrow against is your profit-sharing plan. A typical plan might let you borrow between 50 and 75 percent of the money in your account, and the interest charges can be as low as 10 percent or as high as the prevailing rate of interest. You might, for example, be charged 2 percent above or below the prime rate or the treasury bill rate. To find out if you can borrow against your profit-sharing fund, just make a telephone call to your personnel or employee-benefit department.

There are further advantages to borrowing from a profit-sharing fund, besides the generally low interest rates. Say you have $25,000 in such a fund and borrow $10,000 at 12 percent interest or a cost of $1,200 annually. You still have the full $25,000 in the fund, and you may even have a choice about how that money will be invested. You can use that choice to cover the cost of borrowing. For example, the profit-sharing fund might let you divide the money in your account among stocks, bonds, and a money market fund. If the money market fund pays a rate higher than 12 percent, say, 17 percent interest, you can invest $10,000 of the $25,000 in the money market fund. You will not only recoup the 12 percent you paid for the loan but also earn an extra 5 percent — $500. And that $500 is tax deferred as long as it stays in the fund. Of course, since it goes into the profit-sharing fund, you can't actually use it to pay off the loan. But the cost of the loan will be more than offset by the money you'll make by investing it. You may also earn more than the $1,200 cost by putting your $10,000 loan into a safe investment such as a certificate of deposit yielding 16 or 17 percent. If your CD earns you $1,700 (17 percent interest), you have $500 to split between yourself and Uncle Sam, outright, besides the money that is still accumulating in your profit-sharing account. Remember, this is a *loan* against your assets. The money itself stays in the fund. You can always take out the profit-sharing money directly, but the taxes you will have to pay on it will greatly reduce the amount you can work with, and you will lose the future benefit of the tax deferment on that money.

Uncle Sam

Almost all of us are apprehensive about April 15, the day our taxes are due. But the truth is that most of us pay our taxes much earlier — as we earn our salaries, through withholding. Some of us get a refund on April 15. The money that is refunded, mind you, is your money; and until April 15, you are merely lending it to Uncle Sam. But he is not always a generous uncle; he takes your money and doesn't pay you interest.

It doesn't have to be that way. You see, the amount of money that is withheld from your salary check is determined by the number of dependents you claim. Most people claim only their actual number of dependents. But you can legally claim any number you want. If you claim ten dependents, it is probable that no federal income tax will be deducted from your salary. Of course, April 15 will arrive sooner or later, and on that day accounts must be settled. The new tax law actually penalizes you for underpaying your taxes; but if you anticipate a refund, you can easily estimate the number of dependents you will need to claim in order to avoid overpayment. By the way, Uncle Sam will not penalize you for underestimating money earned from bonuses, commissions, raises or investment gains. Don't let Uncle Sam make money on your money (refunds). Until April 15, you can invest that money safely — in a money market fund, for example — and earn interest on it. A money market fund would in fact be the best investment for this purpose, because you can always take your money out when you want it — in this case, April 15.

Besides keeping your hands on part of Uncle Sam's tax money while it is legally yours, you can also reduce the amount Uncle Sam gets in the end. For that, see "Other People's Money," coming up.

Grants, Scholarships, and Boondoggles

Many federal, state, municipal and private agencies offer qualified people or their dependents a remarkable assortment of grants and loans. And a large number of foundations exist solely to offer scholarships. The loans not only carry low interest rates but can also be repaid over quite a long time. The grants and scholarships are free — outright gifts.

If you are eligible for this kind of money and don't claim it, you are throwing money out of the window. Yet in 1980, 43 percent of the scholarships offered in the United States went unused simply because so many people didn't know they existed and therefore didn't apply for them. To learn how and where to apply for tuition loans, grants, and scholarships, see Section IV ("Cost Savings").

Other People's Money — Borrowing

Whenever you borrow money, you literally buy it. Sometimes you can buy it from "inside" sources — parents, other relatives, friends, employers — people you know personally. We'll consider these inside sources later in the chapter. Most often, you have to buy money from an "outside" source, an institution that specializes in lending money — a bank, for instance.

"Outside" Sources

In essence, lending institutions are just stores that sell money. The price they charge for that money is called *interest,* a percentage of what you borrow. Just as other kinds of stores often sell the same products at different prices, so different lending institutions charge different rates of interest for the same loans. In fact, even the same kinds of lending institutions — two savings banks, for example — often charge different rates. And different banks, like different clothing stores, sell different products. One bank, for example, may offer personal loans, whereas another may not; or it may permit you to repay your loans over a longer period of time than the other bank.

When you want to borrow money from an outside source, be choosey. Visit several different kinds of lending institutions, and tell their loan officers what you want. Avoid doing what most people do: automatically applying for a loan at the same bank where they have an account and accepting — without a second thought — the rate that bank offers. After shopping around, if you find a bank whose rates are more attractive, you may want to switch some of your accounts to it; banks prefer to lend to their own depositors. Before you transfer your funds, however, tell an officer at your present bank why you are abandoning it. Most people don't realize that interest charges are often negotiable, and many banks will accept a lower rate of interest rather than lose a good customer.

Approaching a bank for a loan can be intimidating. But it becomes less intimidating as you gain experience. Remember that banks exist to lend money: they would collapse without customers. Loan officers are happy to talk with potential new customers, just as anyone else who has a product to sell is happy to discuss his wares with a prospective buyer.

Most banks have their own standards for determining anyone's creditworthiness and how much credit to extend. Don't assume that if one bank won't loan you money, the others won't either. Shop around; visit at least three banks in your neighborhood and talk with their loan officers. And when you talk, remember that you can negotiate with banks. Some bank officers may even bend over backwards to help you, especially if you are or have been a good customer.

As we've already seen, it's relatively simple to get a line of credit from a bank; so much so that this is the easiest way to borrow small sums of money ($500 to $5,000). You pay nothing to maintain a line of credit until you actually use it; and it is available instantly: you don't have to sign additional applications or wait for processing. Money is sometimes hardest to get when you need it most, so build up all the lines of credit you can. Getting a regular bank loan may be somewhat more difficult. Allow plenty of time when you apply for one; lending institutions are allowed 30 days from the point when you file an application to notify you of their decision.

Do all of your shopping and homework beforehand. Investigate the interest rates and terms offered by banks and other lending institutions in your area. Find out if they have specific restrictions, such as requiring applicants to have worked a certain number of years at their present jobs or to have lived at their current addresses for a specific length of time. Some expect a minimum down payment for a specific type of loan. Be prepared to discuss your budget in detail; lending institutions want to be assured that you can carry the debt safely.

Make sure that all of your other credit accounts are up to date and in good standing before you apply. This doesn't mean you must pay up all of your past debts, but you must be paid up on all the installments which are due. And you must be prepared to tell the lender about your current obligations: the dollar amounts of your initial loans, the current balances, and how much you pay each month. Never ask the loan officers not to check into a particular credit reference; in most cases, they'll look into that one first, and perhaps even assign undue weight to it.

Feel free to consult the loan officers on other financial matters; giving such advice is part of their job, and they might be able to solve some of your other money problems or to recommend sources and choices you don't know about.

Expect the loan officers to suggest that you buy life or loan insurance to cover your loan, so that if you die before it is completely repaid, the insurance will pay off the remaining balance. This prevents your heirs from inheriting your debt. Buying such insurance is inexpensive and makes good sense, but it is rarely required by law. You do have the choice of refusing — politely, of course.

Last but not least, having a good relationship with a local bank or lending institution can be useful to you in the future, when you may want a mortgage or some other service it provides. Banks always prefer to do business with people they know.

The person who said "Banks won't lend you money until they are convinced that you don't need it" simply had not done his homework or his shopping.

Let's now consider the various kinds of outside sources.

Credit Unions

When you decide to borrow from an outside money source, approach your credit union first. Credit unions are nonprofit lending organizations generally affiliated with social or religious groups or with corporations, labor unions, or educational institutions. Because they do not attempt to make a profit, they generally charge less for their money than do other kinds of lending institutions. To qualify for a loan, in most cases all you have to do is join the sponsoring organization; some credit unions, however, have additional requirements. Access to the credit union is reason enough for joining the group; but membership usually entitles you to other benefits as well, such as low-cost life insurance and health care.

One point to remember, by the way, is that you may already belong to a sponsoring organization, without knowing it. There are more than 23,500 federally chartered credit unions across the country serving 35 to 40 million people. Still, many people don't even know that credit union benefits are available to them. Sometimes this ignorance strikes close to home. A couple of years ago, when my father mentioned to me that he needed to borrow $5,000 to help a nephew, I mentioned credit unions as a possible source. He shrugged and said that he was self-employed and therefore didn't have access to one. After five minutes of questioning and four phone calls, we unearthed no fewer than three credit unions available to him: one from a labor union he belonged to, one connected with a religious society, and still another affiliated with the university where he was teaching at night.

Credit union loans are easy to get, in that you usually don't need a credit history or a minimum salary. All you need is an affiliation with the credit union's sponsoring organization. Contact your college, alumni association, corporate personnel office, labor union, religious organization, social group or veterans' association; they may all have established credit unions that are available to you. And don't forget the low-cost loan insurance and life insurance that may be available through the organization as well. And here is further good news: recent changes in federal law have broadened the kinds of loans that credit unions may make and have substantially increased the amount they may lend.

So make those phone calls, or write to:

Office of the Administrator
National Credit Union Administration
1776 G Street N.W.
Washington, DC 20456

Commercial Banks

Commercial banks specialize in checking accounts and in business loans. But they also make loans to ordinary borrowers — loans whose terms and costs may vary widely.

Simple loans. These are repayable in a lump sum on a specified due date.

Installment loans. These, on the other hand, are paid back in regular monthly or quarterly installments, generally over a period of one to three years.

Balloon loans. Like installment loans, balloon loans are paid in installments. But the last payment is much larger than the others — perhaps 20 to 50 percent of the whole loan. A balloon loan makes sense if you think you will be in a better financial position at a particular point in the future than you are now.

Secured loans. Collateral is anything you offer as security for a loan — stocks, bonds, savings accounts, the cash value of your life insurance, and so on. A secured loan is a loan granted on the security of collateral, which the lender has the right to take and sell if you do not repay the debt. "Collateralizing" a loan usually reduces the interest rate you are charged for it. But your collateral, or at least a part of it, may be "frozen" for the duration of the loan.

Automobile loans. This is a specific kind of installment loan in which the car itself serves as collateral.

Check overdraft loan, or "line of credit." Some banks allow you to write checks in amounts greater than your balance, up to a prearranged limit. The amount that you are permitted to borrow is called your *line of credit* — a very handy thing to have, since it allows you to get a loan simply by writing a check. The bank charges you interest only on the amount of the overdraft, and in most cases rounds this sum off to the nearest hundred dollars. The line of credit itself, for however long you maintain it, costs you nothing until you use it.

Mortgages. In general, commercial banks are not as interested in mortgages as are savings banks, but some may provide them as a service to special clients.

Student loans. Most commercial banks issue special loans for college students — *student loans,* as they are called — some of which are subsidized by the federal government. In the latter case, the bank charges the government the regular interest rate, but the borrower pays only a part of the cost and the government picks up the rest. At the moment, the cost to the borrowers (students or their parents) is 14 percent. But there are hints that the government may change this policy for the 1982-83 school year.

Savings Banks, and Savings and Loan Associations

Savings banks exist in only twelve of the fifty states, mostly in the Northeast. Savings and loan associations, on the other hand, are found in all fifty states. These two kinds of institutions are roughly similar, but they are chartered under different laws. Both make loans — chiefly first and second mortgages and home improvement loans, though in some states savings banks make personal loans, too. Right now (1982), savings banks and savings and loan associations must generally — by law — charge lower interest rates than commercial banks do. But that won't necessarily be true when you go shopping for a loan. The laws and regulations governing these institutions are changing fast, mainly because the Reagan administration hopes to promote free trade and competition among banks by reducing the regulatory burdens of the past thirty to forty years.

Second-Mortgage Companies

Just what is a second mortgage anyway? Suppose you bought

your house ten years ago for $50,000. You put up $10,000 as the down payment and took out a $40,000 mortgage on the rest. In the intervening years you have paid off $10,000 of the mortgage, so only $30,000 remains outstanding. But something else has happened in those ten years, too: the value of the house has tripled to $150,000. You can now take out a loan, a *second mortgage,* on up to 80 or 85 percent (depending on the state where you live) of the current value of the house, minus the amount outstanding from your original mortgage — that is, if you meet the income requirements. For the house in the example, 80 percent of $150,000 (current assessed valuation), minus the $30,000 you still owe on your first mortgage, comes to $90,000.

This money is yours to spend or invest, but you must make sure you keep up your payments on both mortgages; repossession of a house is not a very pleasant experience. And second-mortgage companies may have extra fees, or "charges," that add up and may make such loans more expensive. People who want to refinance their homes or get second mortgages should start by approaching the institutions that hold their first mortgages. But *do* shop around. Interest rates on second mortgages can vary by as much as 5 percent among different banks and 8 percent among various mortgage companies.

Small-Loan (or Finance) Companies

A number of small-loan (or finance) companies are called "industrial loan companies" because they got their start by lending money to industrial workers. Some states place an upper limit on the amount these companies can lend to any one person at any one time, a limit (depending on the state) between $1,000 and $1,500. In certain ways, the terms of small-loan companies are relatively easy: they may, for example, give you an unusually long time to repay. But their interest charges may be two or three times higher than those of banks or savings and loan associations. Their customers tend to be people who cannot borrow money anywhere else because they have poor credit ratings or none at all. In fact, almost anyone can borrow $500 at a small-loan company.

So far, so good. The problem is that it's next to impossible to make money with such a loan. You see, their rates of interest can run as high as 36 percent a year, and even higher; and most borrowers take three to five years to repay. Suppose you borrow $1,000 at 35 percent interest for three years. At the end of those three years, the total interest you have paid could be as high as $1,050 — more than the amount of the loan! But it may be that the only figure the company has quoted you is your monthly payment of $56.44, which sounds reasonable enough.

Some small-loan companies charge you interest only on the declining balance of the loan, which reduces your total cost somewhat in spite of the high rate.

Executive Finance Companies

These outfits specialize in making loans, by mail, to people whose income averages $25,000 to $50,000; and they usually grant loans of between $7,500 and $25,000. Executive finance companies find customers by placing ads in local newspapers and often check borrowers' qualifications by asking for copies of their latest income tax returns. Executive finance companies rarely demand collateral, so they tend to charge high interest rates, ranging from 24 to 45 percent, depending on the company and on the borrower's circumstances.

Stockbrokers

Companies that sell stocks and other securities (such as bonds and treasury bills) are willing to lend clients money to help them buy those securities. Buying a stock, a bond, or a treasury bill in this way is called *buying on margin* or maintaining a margin account. A margin account is an instant, collateralized (backed) loan. It is backed by the value of the security assets (stocks, bonds, cash) in your account.

The amount that stockbrokers can lend to clients is limited by federal law to 75 percent of the price — a "75 percent margin" — in the case of a listed common stock, 70 percent for a corporate bond, and 90 percent for treasury bills and government notes and bonds. Some brokerage firms, however, reduce these limits in order to protect themselves and their clients' interests.

Buying on margin is full of both risks and advantages. Say you buy 100 shares of a stock selling at $10 a share. You buy it on 50 percent margin — in other words, you put up $500 cash and the broker lends you the other $500 at 20 percent interest. After one year the value of the stock goes up by 50 percent, to $15 a share. You have now made $500. Even after you deduct the $100 interest charge, you still have $400, an 80 percent pretax profit on your investment of $500. If all your investments go this well, you'll soon be rich. Had you invested $1,000 of your own money (instead of borrowing $500), your pretax profit would have been only 50 percent.

The story doesn't always have a happy ending, however. If the stock goes down 50 percent, to $5 a share, the total market value of your investment is only $500. Now, this broker only allows you a 50 percent margin on stocks. But at this moment he is giving you a 100 percent margin; to put it differently, the $500 loan (margin) equals 100 percent of the stock's value. To restore the 50 percent margin, you will have to come up with another $500; and if you do not, the broker can sell the stock. In reality, of course, the stock will lose value little by little, and as it does so you will get "margin calls" for whatever amount it will take to restore the 50 percent margin. Even though by federal law you are allowed up to a 75 percent margin on listed stocks, the broker may allow you less, and many don't consider stock selling at less than $10 as good collateral. In that case, if the stock price goes below $10 a share, they will automatically require additional collateral. In any case, when your stock goes down to $5 a share, you've lost $250 on what you had bought on margin, plus all of the interest you've paid for the use of the marginal loan — and that interest may be from 1 to 5 percent higher than the prime rate.

Pawnbrokers

When people are desperate for small amounts of money and

own something with an established market value, the pawnbroker will take that object as collateral and lend them 25 to 50 percent of its value. It is the pawnbroker, by the way, who decides the value. In return for the money, the pawnbroker charges interest — usually on the high side, ranging from 36 to 50 percent — and keeps whatever has been "pledged" (handed over as collateral). Should the borrower fail to redeem the pledge (that is, pay the amount borrowed) at a specified time, the pawnbroker can put it up for sale. If you think you might not be able to redeem a pledge on time, you should simply sell outright to a dealer. You will almost certainly get more money that way, and you won't have to pay interest on it. Of course, if something you own is really valuable, you may be able to use the article itself as collateral for a bank loan. Pawnbrokers are a source of loans, but a source that should be used only in dire emergencies, when you have no alternative. If you do borrow from a pawnbroker, be sure you understand his terms very clearly, especially if you are pledging something of personal value that you hope to redeem.

Private Investors

Through friends or brokers, or through associates at work, you may be able to find private individuals who lend out their own money at interest. These investors charge slightly higher rates than they could get by putting their money into certificates of deposit, treasury bills, or money market funds; but with such people, you can negotiate the rate of interest and the terms of repayment. For example, some private investors may accept a lower rate of interest in return for the right to share any profits you make with the money you've borrowed.

Uncle Sam

We've already seen that you can retain and invest the money that might otherwise be over-withheld from your salary check to pay income taxes. But you can also keep part of the money that would ordinarily go to Uncle Sam *on* April 15. The key is simply this:

What the government taxes is not your *total* income but your *taxable* income, and the two can be very different. For example, if your interest charges (on loans, mortgages, credit cards, and so on) come to $5,000 in a certain year, that means that your taxable income is less by $5,000 because you can deduct interest costs from it. You are excluding $5,000 from taxation. And since your taxable income is lower, the rate at which it is taxed is also lower, so you are helping yourself to Uncle Sam's money in two ways.

Another way to reduce your taxable income is to put your money into a tax-deferred investment plan such as an IRA (individual retirement account) or, if you are self-employed, a Keogh plan. This money is not taxed until you retire, and neither is the interest you make on it, so you can go on and on investing and earning interest on pretax earnings. Suppose, for example, that you are in the 50 percent top-dollar tax bracket (that is, your top-dollar earnings are taxed at a rate of 50 percent). You invest $1,000 in a 15 percent certificate of deposit under an IRA plan. In the first place, by investing the money in an IRA plan, you save $500 in taxes on that $1,000. In the second place, you keep all of the $150 you earn in interest, not just the $75 you'd be left with after taxes if you had bought that CD outside of an IRA. You are in the 50 percent tax bracket (for this example), so in effect you got 30 percent interest, since, if the investment had been taxable, you would have had to earn $300 (30 percent) to keep $150.

There's one catch: you must reinvest the $150, or it *will* be taxed. But reinvesting it really benefits you, not Uncle Sam, since the next time around you will be earning interest on $1,150 and keeping all that interest. You'd be surprised how quickly money can build up in this way. Yes, at some time in the future — when you decide to withdraw the money rather than reinvest it — you will have to pay taxes. But if you wait until after retirement, your tax bracket will probably be much lower. You can withdraw the money after age 59½, but if you need it sooner you will have to pay a 10 percent penalty, in addition to taxes. But at today's interest rates you can make enough to offset that 10 percent penalty in the first year of investing. And in the meantime you are making money with Uncle Sam's money, and making it much more quickly than you could have made it with your own. Remember that $500 of your initial $1,000 was working for you only because you were investing your money under a tax-deferred plan.

Credit and Charge Cards

The general public confuses two kinds of plastic cards by using the terms "credit card" and "charge card" interchangeably. The two are really quite different. True credit cards (like Visa and Mastercard) let you charge merchandise on credit and also let you borrow money. In most cases, when you charge merchandise on a credit card, you don't start paying interest (generally 18 to 20 percent) until the end of a full billing cycle (usually thirty days from the date on your bill); if you pay before then, your charges are interest free. But when you use a credit card to borrow money, you pay interest (usually 18 to 24 percent) from the day the money is borrowed until the date it is repaid.

All credit cards have predetermined spending (and borrowing) limits, set individually for each customer. When you have used up that spending limit, you cannot use the card until you have paid off part or all of the debt.

The other kind of plastic card is a charge card (for example, American Express, Carte Blanche, and Diners Club). Charge cards do not have predetermined spending limits and are therefore preferred for business and travel. But when you use a charge card, you must pay the entire amount as soon as you get the bill. Because there is no "credit" per se, there are no interest charges. And you can't borrow money with a charge card unless a bank (not the company that issues the card) gives you a line of credit that is attached to the charge card; for example, the American Express Gold card. (If you use one of these cards to borrow money, it is the bank that is making you the loan.) You can usually cash personal checks more easily using a charge card as personal verification, but that's not borrowing; it's just a means to quick access to your own cash.

Other Outside Sources

You may wonder why I don't mention how to get access to the "easy" loans advertised in newspapers and magazines and/or on television and radio. Nor do I mention bill consolidators or any other source that does not screen its credit candidates. The reason is that I want to discourage any of you from using those sources. Because they do not screen applicants carefully they face a much higher default rate on repayment of loans. In order to compensate for their increased risk and, therefore, costs, they charge much higher interest rates than conventional lenders. These loans may be easy to get, but they will turn out to be very costly in the long run.

Inside Sources

Shakespeare said, "Neither a borrower nor a lender be." The standard interpretation of this is "Don't ask for a loan, and don't give one." But Shakespeare was living in the sixteenth century, when lending was rather a precarious business. Today's world is greatly changed.

To borrow money, you don't necessarily have to deal with institutions. Borrowing from friends or relatives *can* work out if the terms of the loan are structured properly. Otherwise, this type of loan can lead to bitter feelings or broken friendships. Putting a personal relationship in jeopardy through borrowing is rarely worth the cost. But you can eliminate or at least reduce the problems that can arise in this kind of borrowing.

Parents

Borrowing money from parents can be one of the easiest ways of getting a loan — but only if your parents can afford to make it. If lending you money would force them to give up their vacation, or eat more cheaply, or change their life-style in any way, they cannot afford it. And remember that the interest you offer them should be just as fair to them as it is to you.

The great advantage of getting money from your parents is not so much lower interest rates but the likelihood that your parents will be far more tolerant about late payments than anyone else would be. And they will often accept payment in a lump sum plus interest.

What holds for parents holds also for other relatives. If they have money to lend, they can be good sources of credit. But avoid family disputes; pay back promptly.

Friends

From a purely financial standpoint, friends, like relatives, are a good source of money — again, if they can afford to lend it. But the financial standpoint is not the only consideration. Borrowing from friends can strain your friendships, even if you pay back every cent you owe, with interest, on time.

Employers

Some employers are willing to advance employees money against their salaries, and many such employers charge little or no interest. But they may want to know things you might not want to tell them — the purpose of the loan, for example. Should you spend the money instead of investing it, you will eventually be faced with a payless payday, without a reserve to make up the difference. If you aren't making enough to live on, borrowing from your employer is no solution; it just makes things worse.

When I started my own business, I took out a number of personal loans. In each case I signed a note that read, "X lends Susan Bondy $5,000 for six months at a rate of return of 1 percent more than the current treasury bill [or money market fund, CD, or prime lending] rate. The principal will be paid in full, with interest, six months from today." The particular instrument (money market fund, CD, and so on) on which the interest was calculated was selected on the basis of how the lender would otherwise have used the money I was borrowing. Some of my friends invested in treasury bills, so I paid them 1 percent more than that rate. Had they lent me money out of their money market mutual fund, I would have paid them 1 percent more than that rate.

If your inside sources really don't need the money you propose to borrow, they might accept a rate of return that will just barely exceed the rate of inflation. You can determine that rate by checking the fluctuations of the consumer price index, one measure of inflation. Add one or two percentage points to the published figure. After you agree on a rate of interest, decide whether to repay the money in monthly installments or at the end of the period in a lump sum. If you plan to invest in the no-risk or low-risk strategies, you might further reduce your costs by offering to share your profits — perhaps 5 to 25 percent of the net gain. Sharing promotes goodwill and can even make it easier to borrow from the same source later on.

Should you have trouble meeting a payment due to one of your personal sources, get in touch immediately and explain why honestly. Ask for more time, and offer more money as a compensation for your tardiness. You might also offer to pay a portion of the payment right away. Remember, "insiders" are an excellent source of money, and you want to keep on their good side. More important, though, are the love, devotion, and good communications you want to enjoy with your friends and relatives. Once they are lost, no amount of money can replace them.

As for employers, when you borrow against your salary, you are borrowing your own money, so this may be relatively simple. If you ask your employer for a regular loan, however, follow the same procedures you would use in borrowing from friends and family. But remember that you are more likely to be turned down, and that your employer might want to know what you plan to do with the money.

Credit Histories and Credit Ratings

People complain about credit, joke about credit, and declare to the world that they do not need credit. But they do, and credit is no joking matter. Credit is not just the ability to borrow cash, important though that undoubtedly is. Without credit or a credit card, you cannot buy a house or, in most states, rent a car. You would also find it hard to buy a car, to cash a check or pay by check, or to get ready cash when you're away from home.

Also, many major employers look into your credit history before hiring you, in order to gain insight into your financial reliability and responsibility. Most major rental agencies ask for a credit history before letting you sign a lease; they want to be sure they will get their rent each month, and on time. Many utility companies — gas, electric, water, telephone — forego deposits from applicants who have good credit histories. For these reasons and many more, you must carefully guard and nurture a good credit history and rating, assets that can be worth a lot of money to you.

Credit histories and credit ratings are the keys to getting credit, for unless they are satisfactory most major forms of credit, including loans, are closed to you. A credit history is simply a listing of the credit that has been extended to you in the past and a record of the manner in which you have handled that credit. A credit rating is an assessment of your creditworthiness that is based on your credit history. Both the history and the resultant rating are compiled by specialized credit agencies.

Lenders judge creditworthiness in two ways: your ability to pay and your willingness to pay. Your *ability* to pay is judged on the basis of your current salary, potential earnings, and other sources of income; your asset base; and your current loans outstanding and/or the monthly payment on your current debt. Sometimes a person whose credit history is excellent is turned down for credit because his current level of outstanding debt is too high for his income or because his income has declined.

Your *willingness* to pay debts can be determined by checking your credit history. A credit history includes the source of each loan, its amount, the collateral (if any) you offered for it, the cosigner if any, and how the loan was paid back. Ability to pay and willingness to do so are quite different. The credit histories for many wealthy people show that they do not meet their obligations promptly; and of course lenders regard such people, for all their money, as poor credit risks.

Most credit agencies have four major repayment categories:

1. Paid back satisfactorily, in full and on time — the best.

2. Paid back slowly — which, while not very good, is not a disaster.

3. Collected by an agency or a lawyer — this is bad news. Most lenders have to pay between 25 and 50 percent of the amount collected to the agency or lawyer.

4. Not collected — the worst. It's hard to recover from this rating, because negative credit information remains on the record (by law) for seven years. Personal bankruptcy stays on the record even longer: ten years.

Some credit bureaus, in addition, give you a credit rating based on your credit history. Ratings may be on a scale of 1 to 10, 1 to 100; a letter code of A, B, C, D; or descriptive words like "Excellent," "Good," or "Poor." Not all credit bureaus calculate credit ratings. Some just provide a listing of past and present credit sources.

A bad credit history or credit rating may result from your own mishandling of past credit, but it can also be caused by errors in your credit files. You can check this out, because, by law, all lenders who deny you credit must tell you why. This is required in order to prevent discrimination on illegal grounds such as sex, age, marital status, religion, race, color, and national origin. The three most common reasons for being denied credit are:

- insufficient income,
- a poor credit history, and
- lack of a credit history.

If your income is too low, you will just have to ask for a raise or get a better-paying job. But if you suspect that your credit history is inaccurate, you can investigate it and even get it corrected.

Besides telling you why you were turned down, the lender must give you the name of the credit agency that supplied the report leading to your rejection. You can request to see your credit report, at no cost, within thirty days of being turned down. In fact, you can get your credit report even if you haven't been turned down, but in that case you will have to pay $2 to $10 for the privilege. And since there are over 200 credit agencies, it is not practical to try to inspect all reports regularly.

When you do inspect a report, first look for actual errors — a repaid debt listed as outstanding, for example; or an entry that just isn't yours. Then look for omissions — unrecorded credit — and not only omitted loans, but also lines of credit, mortgages, and so on. Now try to find "unfair" entries, such as charges posted to your account before you received the merchandise, or payments that were excusably late because of illness or unemployment but not so recorded.

Should you find such problems, point them out to the credit agency immediately. The agency must then check out your complaints; if you are right, they must correct errors and omissions, add permanent explanatory notes to unfair entries, and send the corrected report to you. If the report contains an actual error, the agency must also send the corrected report to anyone who has received the old one.

Discrimination. In addition to the illegal discrimination I mentioned, you cannot be discriminated against because of the source of your income. Transfer payments (welfare or child support, for example), social security, pensions and alimony must be considered as income. A creditor may, however, take into account the stability and longevity of the income: child support will end when the child reaches a certain age; alimony payments are only as reliable as the alimony payer.

If you suspect discrimination on one or more of the grounds mentioned above, you have a simple means of redress: Write a letter to the president or chairman of the lending institution involved and send a copy by registered mail, return receipt requested, to the regulatory agency (see below) that enforces these antidiscriminatory regulations. Describe your complaint clearly and concisely. Include all the facts — names, dates, places. Most of the time, you will get a satisfactory answer within a week or two, because lending institutions and banks prefer to avoid litigation or investigation by a government agency. If your problem is not addressed satisfactorily, you can sue for actual damages plus up to $10,000 in punitive damages. Below is a list of the agencies to which you should send complaints about discrimination (or any other complaint, for that matter):

Lender	*Regulatory Agency*
National banks	Consumer Affairs Office of the Comptroller of the Currency Washington, DC 20219 Telephone: (202) 566-2000
Store, dealer, finance company, small-loan company	Bureau of Consumer Protection Federal Trade Commission Washington, DC 20580
Nonmember insured banks	Office of Bank Customer Affairs Federal Deposit Insurance Corp. Washington, DC 20420 Telephone: (202) 389-4427
Savings and loan association	Local Federal Home Loan Bank Board's supervisory agent *or* Office of General Counsel Federal Home Loan Bank Board Washington, DC 20552 Telephone: (202) 377-6000

Lender	*Regulatory Agency*
Federal credit union	National Credit Union Administration 2025 M Street N.W. Washington, DC 20456 Telephone: (202) 254-9800
State-chartered credit union	Your state department of banking *or* finance department

Establishing a Credit History

If the agency reports that you have an "insufficient" credit history, it simply means that the agency has few credit listings for you. Get to work immediately to correct that situation. The simplest way to establish a credit history is to get a credit card or a charge card in your own name — your name on your parents' card doesn't count. It is easier to get the cards of some retail stores and gasoline chains than others, and different banks (which issue credit cards) have different income and residency requirements, so if you get turned down by one, just apply somewhere else. In addition, you can take out a loan that is repayable over six months (shorter loans generally are not picked up by credit agencies). The cheapest and easiest source for such a loan is your credit union. As was mentioned earlier, in most cases a credit union's only requirement for a loan is membership in one of its sponsoring organizations. You might also choose to take out an installment loan from a bank. For a first loan, the bank may ask you to provide collateral or a co-signer.

Married women should establish credit histories in their own names while they are married. (Don't wait until you get divorced, separated, or widowed, when you may need money right away.) Since 1977, credit granted to married couples is automatically placed on the credit histories of both husband and wife, but a married woman may have to ask pre-1977 creditors to make sure that joint credit is reflected on her own credit history.

Remember that taking out a loan does not establish a credit rating or a credit history; paying back the loan does that. So college and educational loans cannot help you create a credit rating until six months after you begin to repay them. This is usually twelve months after graduation, so the borrower must wait a year and a half to establish a credit rating with such loans.

Your creditworthiness comprises your ability to pay debts plus your willingness to do so. Sometimes you can't do much about your ability to pay, but you *can* establish your willingness, and thus uphold your reputation as a borrower. A favorable credit history is a precious asset.

Charting Your Money Sources

Now that you know the sources of money, it's time to take stock of your own position. To do that, you need a system, one that tells you how much is available to you from each source, and also the cost of obtaining it. Your system should be updated frequently — at least once a year and preferably twice — to help you find new sources of money and to keep track of its changing costs, for interest rates do change. On the following pages you will find charts that will help you to list your current sources of money and to track down and investigate possible future sources. At the end the columns are explained. Make sure you fill in each entire line. It may even take a few phone calls to gather information, but this is crucial for the success of the strategies. You will also be gathering information that may be invaluable in your future.

MONEY SOURCES

Sources	(1) Total Amount	(2) Amount Used	(3) Amount Available for Use	(4) Annual Percentage Rate	(5) Other Charges	(6) Total Costs
Your own money						
Example: life insurance cash value	$20,000	-0-	$20,000	6%	NONE	6%
"Inside"						
Parents	$10,000	$5,000	$ 5,000	14%	NONE	14%
"Outside"						
Credit line	$ 5,000	$1,000	$ 4,000	18%	NONE	18%

Column (1) represents the total amount you have available at any one time.

(2) represents the amount, if any, used already — for example, current charges on a credit card.

(3) represents the difference, if any, between columns 1 and 2.

(4) represents the rate of interest for each loan.

(5) represents other charges, such as points, penalties, and administrative charges.

(6) represents the sum of columns 4 and 5: in other words, the total cost of each loan.

POTENTIAL MONEY SOURCES

Sources	(1) Total Amount	(2) Amount Used	(3) Amount Available for Use	(4) Annual Percentage Rate	(5) Other Charges	(6) Total Costs
Your own money						
"Inside"						
"Outside"						

Column (1) represents the total amount you have available at any one time.

(2) represents the amount, if any, used already — for example, current charges on a credit card.

(3) represents the difference, if any, between columns 1 and 2.

(4) represents the rate of interest for each loan.

(5) represents other charges, such as points, penalties, and administrative charges.

(6) represents the sum of columns 4 and 5: in other words, the total cost of each loan.

SECTION III
INVESTMENT VEHICLES EXPLAINED

B efore you can make money through investments, you have to understand the kinds of investment opportunities and vehicles that are available to you. These investments include stocks, bonds, short-term (or liquid) investments, options, mortgages, and collectibles.

Stocks

Stocks represent shares in the ownership of a company. Owning a share means owning a part of the company, the good *and* the bad, the losses as well as the profits. If the corporation makes money, you participate in the profits; if the company loses money, your shares may become worthless, although you are not liable for its debts.

Of course, since we are talking about corporations, the losses to shareholders are limited by definition to their investment in the company.

Useful to any discussion of stocks and bonds is the following breakdown of who has prior claim (first "dibs") on the assets of a corporation in the event of bankruptcy.

1. U.S. government — taxes.
2. Employee payroll.
3. Pension fund — up to one-third of the net worth of the company.

4. Outside creditors, including commercial paper holders.
5. Bondholders.
6. Preferred stockholders and convertible preferred stock-holders.
7. Common stockholders.

The above list defines the degree of risk inherent in these securities. It will help you determine the likelihood of getting your money back in case of bankruptcy of the corporation. The higher the priority of the investment, the better your chances are of getting your money back.

Why Do Stock Prices Change?

Stocks are bought and sold at "auctions" — the world's many stock markets — where sellers get together with buyers to reach mutually agreeable prices.

The price of a stock reflects the best information that is available about the company and about the economy at the time of the trade. When there are more buyers for a stock than there are shares for sale, the price moves up. When there are more people who want to sell a stock than there are purchasers for it, the price goes down. The greater the number of informed buyers and sellers, the more accurate the current price of the stock; that is, the more precisely will the price of the stock reflect the value of the shares. Why? Because the moment the price of the stock moves "out of line," some astute investor will capitalize on the discrepancy between what the stock is worth and what it is selling for. As more and more people track a stock, the more quickly its price will adjust to new information (such as increases in earnings and dividends, new products introduction, new markets, a change in management, changes in economic outlook, etc.). Given this attention, the market price of a company's stock is indeed the stock's value at any given time. The problem is that the market is an efficient way of pricing only those stocks that are widely held, closely followed, and actively traded. But in many cases a company's capitalization (the number of shares times the price per share) is too small for its shares to be attractive to the large institutional investors who are often responsible for whatever efficiency the market does have. Other stocks are "closely held" — that is, owned by a few individuals. If these stocks are not traded frequently, their prices may not adjust quickly, and they may present unusual opportunities for unusual returns — either unusually high or unusually low.

The stock market reacts to guesses, opinions, and projections, as well as new information and facts. What people *think* the market or a particular stock will do is not necessarily what will happen. No wonder picking stocks is such a tricky business.

Does this mean that the market price of stock results from mere speculation? Some people think so, and of course in a sense it is a speculation about the future. But perhaps the following historical facts will shed some light on the attraction of common stocks for so many investors.

Over the last fifty years, stocks have returned 6 to 7 percent in real terms — that is, over and above inflation. During the same period, bonds have returned 2 to 3 percent, with t-bills coming in at ½ to 1 percent above inflation. This has been true not only for those fifty years but also for most cumulative five- and ten-year periods during those fifty years. During "bull" or up markets, stocks have traditionally appreciated in price from 60 percent to over 200 percent. And most of the cocktail party talk is about "winners." Lest you forget the "bear" or down markets, during the last major stock market collapse (January 1973 to September 1974) the average stock lost one-half its value. This may not sound too bad, but if a stock goes down 50 percent, it has to subsequently go up by 100 percent just to get back to where it started from. If a $30 stock goes down by 50 percent, its new price will be $15. At $15 a share it has to double in value (go up by 100 percent) to get back to $30.

Many factors affect the price of a stock. Let's take a closer look at those factors and at the terms that are most frequently used to describe or categorize a stock.

Earnings and Dividends

Earnings are a company's profits. Dividends are the sums the company elects to pay to its shareholders or owners of stock. Generally, dividends are declared quarterly and paid quarterly, although some companies also declare year-end "extras." Dividend rates can go down, but historically they have generally remained the same or risen over time. The higher the dividend payout, the less money the company keeps for internal growth (expansion), external growth (acquisitions), or internal financing (not having to borrow money from outside sources).

In the world of finance, the S-shaped earnings/dividends curve is a term used to describe the relationship among a company's earnings, its dividend payout, and its prospects for future growth and expansion. The curve looks like this:

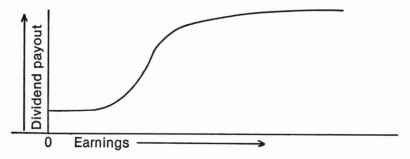

When a company is just starting out (emerging growth), it pays no dividends because it needs the money to finance growth from within. At this point a company may be an exciting but risky candidate for investment. After all, it could also flop. The above curve could easily look like this:

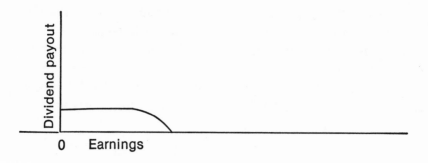

or like this:

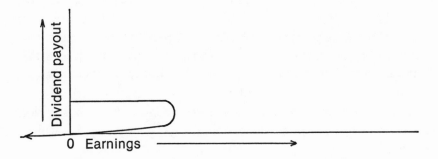

— otherwise known as bankruptcy!

Normally, however, as the company becomes more mature and starts to pay dividends, its earnings growth rate tends to slow down. That doesn't mean that actual earnings decrease, but that the rate at which they are increasing starts to diminish.

Finally the company reaches a "plateau" or mature stage, paying out much of its after-tax earnings to its stockholders in dividends. At this stage, the company will not grow much, and earnings may become more stable. The price of a mature stock will continue to fluctuate, however, because the value of the dividends to investors will change as interest rates change. In addition, the price/earnings multiple that people are willing to pay for this stock may change.

Price-to-earnings ratios. We've already seen that one of the things that can affect a stock's price is its dividends-to-earnings ratio. Another is the ratio between the price of a stock and its earnings — or, to put it another way, the amount of money you have to put up to get a dollar of current earnings. This figure, the price-to-earnings ratio (P/E), is calculated by dividing a stock's current market price by its earnings per share over the last year. A company whose stock earned $4 a share over the past year and now sells for $44 a share has a P/E of 11. To put it yet another way, the stock sells for 11 times its current earnings.

Investors may be willing to pay $11 for each $1 of current

earnings if they believe future earnings or future prices will be higher. Professional investors use estimates of *future* earnings for calculating P/Es on the ground that potential earnings are more important to a prospective buyer than past or present earnings. But, to be useful, such projections have to be reasonably accurate; and even if they are, you can never be sure that other investors have not already discounted (taken into consideration) the expected future growth in earnings into the current purchase price. That is why the price does not always go up when earnings increase.

Let's take that company whose stock sells at $44 a share, whose earnings are $4 a share, and whose current P/E is 11. You estimate that earnings will rise to $5 a share within twelve months, and if the P/E stays at 11, the price should go to $55. It is possible that the projections of future earnings are correct, and that they are already accepted by most investors; that is, the current price of $44 already reflects the expectation of $5-a-share earnings over the next year. If that is true, the price will most likely remain at $44 a share. On the other hand, earnings might rise to $5 at a time when the general market is down and the current overall market P/E has declined. Let's assume that the current market P/E is 9, and that the earnings on our stock are up from $4 to $5. People are not going to be eager to pay $11 for each dollar of earnings — which they would be doing if the stock's price were to go to $55 — when they can buy other stocks and get a dollar of earnings for $9. In this case, the price of our stock might move up to $45 ($5 earning × 9 P/E), an increase of $1 a share.

Price-to-earnings ratios often fluctuate, along with the fortunes of the market and the economy as a whole: as stocks rise, P/Es generally rise with them; and as stocks fall, P/Es generally fall. When a particular company is growing quickly and investors expect that rapid growth to continue, the P/E of the company's stock will tend to rise no matter what is happening to the market as a whole. You can often tell a lot by looking at the history of a company's P/Es and comparing its ups and downs with those of the stock market as a whole. You can get this information from your broker or, in a library, from Standard & Poor's stock guides.

Keep in mind that a stock's P/E ratio will not necessarily return to its previous highs. What is considered high or low at any given time depends very much on current market conditions. When investors get only 5 percent from bonds, they may be willing to pay twenty-five to thirty times earnings for growth companies. Yet when the same bonds yield 13 to 18 percent, the stock market may not be so attractive, and growth stocks may be priced at only ten to fifteen times earnings. So P/E ratios, though useful, should not be the only basis for your investment decisions.

You cannot really say that a stock is cheap just because its P/E ratio is low. You have to consider *why* it is low.

For example, utility stocks currently offer investors low prices and high dividends. Sounds like a bargain, doesn't it? But utilities are regulated companies whose earnings are not expected to grow rapidly in the future. If they do decide to expand, they have less capital available from internal sources, so they must borrow from outside sources which are more expensive. For these and other reasons, the price of utilities stock is currently low, relative to past earnings.

Young companies paying low dividends or none at all can usually be expected to grow faster, and this may make them profitable, despite their higher P/Es.

Types of Stock
Besides common stocks, there are other kinds, not to mention rights to purchase stocks.

Preferred stocks are like common stocks except that they get preferred treatment over common stocks on dividends and upon liquidation. Preferred stock generally pays a higher rate per year than the common stock, and the dividend doesn't fluctuate with earnings. Preferred stockholders must receive their full dividend before the common stockholders get a nickel. Preferred dividends remain fixed and are usually cumulative. If the company does not earn a sufficient amount in one year to cover its preferred dividend, it will still owe you this money next year.

Convertibles are bonds or preferred stocks that can be exchanged, within a specified period of time, for a fixed number of shares of the company's common stock. As with regular preferred stock, they generally pay a higher dividend than the common stock, and may present interesting arbitrage possibilities. (Arbitrage is exchanging one investment for another in order to profit from a temporary price discrepancy.)

Rights and warrants. When a company decides to raise more money by selling more stock, the current shareholders may have the first chance to buy. For each share they own, they are given the "right" to buy a fractional part of a new share at a predetermined price. Rights can also be bought or sold in the marketplace, but when they expire they become worthless.

Warrants are issued by companies often in a package deal with certain stocks and bonds. Warrants give you the right to buy additional shares at a specified price and may or may not have an expiration date.

Rights give you an option to buy shares from the company, and warrants give you the right to buy shares directly from the issuer or on the market. Warrants may also be traded on a stock exchange.

The values of rights and warrants are determined by the difference between the exercise price (your predetermined price as a current shareholder) and the current price of the stock; in other words, their value is based on what someone else is willing to pay for them.

Private stocks. Privately held corporations issue stocks, but these shares are generally bought or sold directly through the organization. In most cases, trading with anybody else (an outside party) is prohibited. The price of a share is usually determined by the value of the assets of the company divided by the number of shares outstanding.

Categories of Common Stocks

Growth stocks are shares in companies whose earnings are expected to grow at unusually high rates. Some of these companies may be newly formed or inadequately capitalized, which makes for higher levels of risk.

Blue chips are longtime leaders in an industry. These companies have grown more slowly, but they have generally paid high dividends. When earnings growth slows or the market goes down, the value of these stocks does not generally drop as quickly as that of growth stocks.

A *special situation* may be a good buy, not because the company's history is especially good but because of new developments that are likely to cause the price to rise. During the period that investors expect improving profits, the stock can rise sharply; but at the first sign that things aren't going so well, the price can also collapse.

Stable is a term used to describe the stock of a company whose products are always needed. Such stocks are less sensitive to economic and political changes or pressures. Examples are consumer durables, foods and utilities.

Cyclical stocks are those issued by companies whose earnings and dividends shoot up during economic upturns and decline during recessions. These are typically basic-industry (steels, chemicals, etc.) and housing stocks.

Income stocks are those that have consistently paid a high dividend. Utility stocks are the prime example of high income stocks.

Other Terms

Stock splits. The corporate purpose of a split is to adjust the price of the stock downward in order to attract more investors to the lower, more affordable price. If you own 100 shares at $90 each, a 2-for-1 split leaves you with 200 shares at a market price of $45 each. The total dollar value stays the same. Splits are sometimes accompanied by a dividend increase. If the new lower price does indeed attract more investors, the additional buying pressure may push the price up. However, if the company's earnings or dividends do not improve, any price increase that may follow the stock split will probably dissipate.

Exchanges are places where the major stocks are bought and sold. When you give a buy order to a stockbroker, he sends it to the "floor" of the exchange; there your stock is bought from another broker, whose customer has decided to sell. The exchanges provide well-regulated centers, designed to keep markets liquid and orderly. The exchanges themselves don't own stock.

Market cycles. Among the factors which affect the rise and fall of stock prices is the amount of money available for investment in the stock market, which in turn is influenced by the relative level of interest rates. When interest rates are high, money is attracted out of the stock market and into bonds and government securities where the income is more attractive and the risks appear low. When interest rates fall, fixed-income investments become less attractive and monies flow back into stocks.

Economic cycles. Traditionalists have labeled the four phases of an economic cycle as recession, depression, recovery, and prosperity. Knowing which phase we are currently in and being able to judge its duration can mean great profits for you. But history shows that even the most astute professional investors have not been able to "call the turns" from phase to phase correctly and on a consistent basis.

Diversification and concentration. Putting all your eggs into one basket is the surest way to riches or disaster, depending on the viability of the basket. As a general rule, the less specialized information you have, the more diversified you should be. Whenever you have a large percentage of your assets in one company/industry (through direct ownership of the stock, or a stock-purchase plan, or profit-sharing plans), extra care should be taken to diversify the remaining assets. At times this may have the effect of diluting profits, but it can also avert potential disaster. The perfect instrument for diversification is an index mutual fund which buys and holds a large list of securities, in direct proportion to their weight in a broad index, such as the Standard & Poor's 500.

How to Read Stock Quotations

Reading stock quotations is not so complicated as most people think. To learn how, let's use three fictitious companies that could have been listed on the New York Stock Exchange or the American Stock Exchange.

EXCHANGE NAME

52-Week High	Low	Stock	Div	Yld in %	P/E Ratio	Sales in 100s	High	Low	Last	Chg
4¼	2½	ABC			3	1397	4¼	3¼	4	. . .
13½	10	DEF	.40	3.4	7	57	12¼	11¼	11½	− ½
24¼	14¼	HIJ	1.00	5.1	19	484	22½	19¼	19½	− 2

The 52-week highs and lows are printed only once a week, generally in the Sunday edition of the newspaper. These two columns are particularly informative because they answer two questions:

a. Is the price currently near the 52-week low (has it declined), or is it close to or at the 52-week high (has it had a recent runup)?

b. What is the range in which the stock has traded over the past year? Is it a narrow or a wide range?

The abbreviation of a company's name is followed by the current annual dividend per share, which is based on the latest quarterly or semiannual declaration, unless otherwise noted.

Yld stands for current yield, the annual dividend divided by the current (last) stock price. P/E refers to the price-to-earnings ratio; that is, the number of times by which the company's latest twelve-month earnings must be multiplied to obtain the current stock price. *Sales in 100s* refers to the volume of shares in consolidated trading during the preceding day or week. The *High, Low* and *Last* columns refer to the day's trading prices. A *u* in the *High* column indicates a new 52-week low. *Chg* is the difference — plus, minus, or no change — between the day's last reported price and the previous day's closing price.

An *s* indicates a split or that a stock dividend of 25 percent or more has been paid. In case of a split, the stock's yearly price range and dividend reflect the new stock price. Special or extra dividends are indicated by the following footnotes: a-Also extra or extras. b-Annual rate plus stock dividend. c-Liquidating dividend. e-Declared or paid in the preceding 12 months. g-Dividend and earnings in Canadian money. h-Declared or paid after stock dividend or split-up. j-Paid this year, dividend omitted, deferred, or no action taken at last dividend meeting. k-Declared or paid this year on a cumulative issue with dividends in arrears. n-New issue. p-Paid this year, dividend omitted, deferred, or no action taken at last meeting. r-Declared or paid in the preceding 12 months plus stock dividend. t-Paid in stock in preceding 12 months, estimated cash value on ex-dividend or ex-distribution date.

Other footnotes: cld-Called. x-Ex-dividend: that is, any dividend payable on the stock is payable to the seller, not to the buyer. y-Ex-dividend and sales in full. xdis-Ex-distribution. xr-Ex-rights. xw-Without warrants. ww-With warrants. wd-When distributed. wi-When issued. nd-Next-day delivery. vi-In bankruptcy or receivership or being reorganized under the Bankruptcy Act, or securities assumed by such companies.

There are many stock exchanges, but the three major ones in the United States are the New York Stock Exchange, the American Stock Exchange, and NASDAQ.*

As we've said before, these stocks could have appeared on the American Stock Exchange or the New York Stock Exchange. But they were not on the NASDAQ quotations. Why? Because NASDAQ quotations appear in a different format.

NASDAQ quotations will appear as follows:

Over-the-Counter Quotations
NASDAQ Quotations

	Div.	Sls in 100s	Bid	Asked	Bid Chg
ABB	1.00	22	7¼	7½ +	1/8
CDD	.46	2	22¾	23¼ +	1/4
EFE	.20	2	17	18 +	1/4

ABB is an abbreviation of the company name. This is followed by the current annual dividend, based on the latest declaration. *Sales in 100s* refer to the volume of trading on that day. The next two columns, *Bid* and *Asked,* are respectively the price "bid" to buy the stock and the "asked" price to sell the stock. The *Bid Change* is the difference between the day's last reported price and the previous day's last bid price.

---

*NASDAQ is the National Association of Securities Dealers automatic quotation system. This organization oversees the over-the-counter (OTC) markets, which deal in stocks that are not traded on the other exchanges but are bought and sold through dealers. All dealers making a market in a particular stock enter their prices daily on the NASDAQ computer. Your broker can check the prices on his own desk-top terminal and place your order where the price is best.

Keeping Accurate Records

The table on page 91 will help you to keep track of your purchases and sales. This is important both for tax reasons (you will need to know whether your gains or losses are long-term or short-term) and for performance evaluation (how well you did).

For tax purposes, dividends are taxed as regular income in the year they are received. Capital gains tax and capital loss tax credit apply only on price appreciation and depreciation that have been realized and are reportable in the year of the sale.

Monitoring Price Movements

The worksheet on page 92 will serve you well in Section IV as a discipline for evaluating and therefore cutting losses or taking profits. At regular intervals (not longer than three months), enter the current price of each stock. Prices may be obtained through your newspaper or a broker.

In order to tell whether your investments were successful or not you must know your rate of return. An accurate rate of return is complicated and cumbersome to calculate. An approximation may be computed as follows:

$$ROR = \frac{EMV - BMV - (P - S - I)}{BMV + \dfrac{(P-S-I)}{2}}$$

Where

ROR = Rate of return;

EMV = Ending market value of securities (total);

BMV = Beginning market value of securities;

P = Total purchases for period;

S = Total sales for period;

I = Total income received for period (interest and/or dividends).

STOCK PURCHASES, SALES, AND RETURNS

(1)	(2)	(3)	(4)	(5)	(6)	(7)	(8)	(9)	(10)	(11)	(12)	(13)
Sec. Name	Ex- chge.	Tkr. Sym.	# of Shares	Date Pur.	Pur. Price	Shs. × Pr. Value	Date Sold	Sale Price	Value	Div. Rcd.	Diff. in Value	Long or Short
XYZ	NYSE	XYZ	100	3/21/80	11¼	1,125						
XYZ							4/30/82	20	2,000	100	875	LTG

Column (1): Name of the company (stock).

(2): Exchange it is listed on.

(3): Ticker symbol — that 1 to 5 character symbol that identifies the stock. Your broker uses this symbol to access the price of the stock through an electronic system.

(4): Number of shares. Keep each lot separately. If you buy 100 shares of XYZ Company at 14 and a week later buy another 100 shares at 12, list these two purchases separately.

(5): Date of purchase.

(6): Purchase price of the stock.

(7): Value of purchase (column 4 × column 6).

(8): Sale date.

(9): Sale price of stock.

(10): Value of sale (column 4 × column 9).

(11): Dividend received — total dividends received during the period you were holding the stock.

(12): Principal value change (column 7 minus column 10).

(13): Mark LTG (long-term gain); LTL (long-term loss); STG (short-term gain); STL (short-term loss)

MONITORING PRICE MOVEMENTS

Security Name	Exchange	Tkr. Sym.	# of Shs.	Date Pur.	Purchase Price	Price as of	Price as of	Value	Price as of	Value	Price as of	Value	Price as of	Value	Price as of

A shorter but less accurate estimation is:

$$ROR = \frac{EMV - BMV + I}{BMV + \frac{I}{2}}$$

Options

The right to buy or sell a stock at a particular price within a specified period of time is called an option. The instrument has value only in terms of what someone else is willing to pay for it at any particular point in time.

When you buy a stock, you buy a portion of a company. When you buy a bond, you lend your money to a company, which gives you prior claim to its assets if the firm should go bankrupt.

When you buy an option, however, you merely pay a price for the right to buy and sell the underlying stocks. I keep saying buy and sell, which may sound confusing, so I will define the two basic types of options.

A *call option* gives you the right to buy stock in a company at a prespecified price within a given period of time. A *put option* lets you sell the stock at a particular time for a particular price. A *naked call* or a *naked put* means you buy or sell options without owning the underlying stocks.

A simple example: Stock in the ABC Company currently trades at $40 a share. Your analysis of this company suggests that this price will rise to $50 a share within the months ahead. You want to invest in the stock. In order to buy 100 shares, you need to invest $4,000 plus the broker's commission. You could of course put $2,000 down and buy the stock on a 50 percent margin.

If the stock goes up to $50, you realize a profit of $1,000 before commissions, or a return of 25 percent on your $4,000 investment. If, on the other hand, the stock drops to $30 a share, and you decide to sell, you sustain a loss of $1,000. But besides buying the stock outright, there is another way for you to capitalize on the hoped-for price increase. That is the *right* to buy the stock for a stated price within a certain period of time; or, as it is known, an option.

Based on the same example, you can secure for the next ninety days the right to buy 100 shares of ABC Company at $40 a share. The price you pay for this privilege is called a premium; and on this particular day, the premium to buy an option on 100 shares of ABC Company at $40 costs you $2.

The $40 a share at which you can purchase the stock is called the *strike price*. The ninety-day limit is called the *expiration date*. When the option expires, it becomes worthless. Now let us see what can happen.

If the price goes up to $50, you simply exercise your right or option to buy the 100 shares at $40 each, then turn around immediately and sell them for the market price of $50. Your gain before the commission is $1,000 minus the $200 you paid for the option, or a net pre-tax profit of $800. This represents a 300 percent return on your initial investment of $200. Had you bought the shares outright, you would still have a $1,000 gain before commission; however, this would represent only a 25 percent increase on your $4,000 investment.

Now let us take a look at what will happen if the price goes down to $30 a share within the next ninety days. If you buy the stock outright, you will then be sitting on a $1,000 loss. If you still hold the option, chances are the option price will go down very close to zero. To this extent, your maximum loss on a call option is the amount of your initial investment. Your maximum risk, in this case, is the loss of the $200.

Keep in mind, however, that if you buy the stock outright you will still own it, and it may one day go up again. If you buy the option and hold it to expiration, it becomes worthless. Therefore, if the price is going down quickly, it is expedient that you try to cut your losses. This is particularly important if the option is getting close to its expiration date. If the price of the stock is below the strike price of the option at expiration, the option becomes worthless.

A *put option,* the opposite of a call, is an option to sell the stock at a specific price, called the striking price. In this case you profit if the price of the security falls. Another example: Assume that ABC Company stock sells for $50 a share. You pay $2 a share for the right to sell, or put, 100 shares of ABC Company at $49 each within the next six months. If the stock falls to $47, you can, theoretically, buy ABC Company at that price and resell it through your broker at $49. You pay, of course, the normal brokerage fees. But, in fact, you could also sell your option at a profit — to somebody who hopes that the option price will improve even more.

A covered put option is a conservative investment vehicle that, when used properly, allows you to limit your risk in a stock. For example, you bought ABC at $50 a share, which gave you owner-ship of the underlying stock, and saw it rise to $65 and then begin to fall again. Yet you may not be quite ready to sell out; you think it may turn around and climb again. So you buy puts of $60. The $2 per share cost of buying this particular put gives you an effec-tive price of $58. If the price of the stock rises and you still hold a put, you can sustain quite a loss. There are two ways this can happen.

Let's say that you own the underlying stock, as in the above-mentioned example, which you bought at $50 a share. If you exer-cise your right to sell it at $58, your upward potential is limited. If, however, you bought a naked put (you own put options without owning the underlying shares), the seller has the right to buy the stock from you at $58 a share. Supposing the investor chooses to exercise that right. And if the price goes up to $200 a share, you can bet that investor will! You must then buy the underlying stock at $200 a share and sell it at $58 a share.

As you can see, one of the more risky things you can do is to buy naked put options. The price of a stock can only go down to zero, but it can go up to infinity. The buying and selling of all types of options is just one way to speculate. If you believe strongly in an investment opportunity, you can use put and call options to maxi-mize your returns.

Options and Quotations

You will notice that on any given day there may be three, four, or more 100-share units, or contracts, as they are known, listed with the same strike price but with different expiration dates. The longer the expiration date, the more time you have for the underlying stock to appreciate in line with your expectations. At the same time, a longer option usually means a higher price. However, this slightly higher cost can serve as very cheap insurance against something happening in the short term which you did not expect or desire.

Reading options quotations. As with any quotation, options are far less mysterious at second glance than they seemed at first. Below is an options quotation for a fictitious company.

	Feb.		May		Aug.		NY
	Vol.	Last	Vol.	Last	Vol.	Last	Close
Ensign 25	17	6	13	7	11	7 1/2	32
Ensign 30	22	1/8	17	3 1/4	16	4	32
Ensign 35	19	1 3/8	16	2	13	3	32

By looking at the far left, you find the corporate name — in this case, Ensign. The figure following the corporate name represents the price per share if the investor exercises the option. In other words, an investor could hold a call option with a strike price of $25, $30, $35. The investor could also hold a put option with a strike price of $25, $30, $35. A call option allows its owner to buy the stock at the strike price, and a put option allows its owner to sell the stock at its strike price.

The months given across the top of the quote show the expiration date. With rare exceptions, options fall due on the third Friday of a month. To find the precise date, an investor just checks a calendar. For options expiring on another day, consult your broker.

Investment jargon calls an option by a combination of expiration date, corporate name, and price. Therefore, you have the

February Ensign 25, the May Ensign 30, the August Ensign 35, and so on. There may also be February Ensign 30 and February Ensign 35 options. In other words, there may be a number of contracts expiring on the same day, all worth different strike prices and trading prices.

Under each listed month there are two columns. *Vol.,* an abbreviation of volume, represents the number of contracts traded. According to this quote, seventeen February Ensign 25 contracts changed hands. Since each contract equals 100 shares of stock, a total of 1,700 shares of Ensign stock were involved.

The figure given under *Last* is the closing price, in hundreds, for each contract. Again, referring to the February Ensign 25, we see, under Last, 6. At closing, a contract sold for $600, or $6 for each share of stock.

The last column, on the far right, *N.Y. Close,* indicates the closing price of Ensign stock itself on the New York Stock Exchange. The final price was, we see, $32 per share.

But knowing what options are and being able to read an option quote are not so important as understanding how best to use options for investment gains.

What to Do Before You Buy Options

First, find a company and a broker specializing in options. This gives you access to sophisticated tools to tell you the value of an option. It does not, however, eliminate your need to know everything possible about the company whose options you want to buy. But because prices fluctuate so much in any given week, you are better off having somebody — a broker — monitor the prices on a daily or maybe even an hourly basis. Following your investments so closely can make all the difference between making and losing money.

Also, before you invest in any options, learn as much about options in general as you can. There are two particularly informative booklets available at no charge either from your stockbroker or from the Chicago Board of Options.

To get them by mail, write to the Chicago Board Options Exchange, La Salle at Jackson, Chicago, Illinois 60604 and request *Understanding Options* and *Option Buying Strategies.*

Fixed-Income Investments

Fixed-income investments are loans, except that you are lending money instead of borrowing. Your loan to the issuer becomes a debt for the issuer (a corporation, a bank, or Uncle Sam). Some loans, however, may be liquid — they may be bought or sold on any day — but the value of the loan, or the price of the fixed-income investment, will fluctuate. Some loans are not liquid (i.e., CDs and t-bills) and cannot be sold before maturity unless a willing third-party buyer can be found.

The amount of interest this investment pays is fixed when it is issued, and that interest must be paid regularly until the date the investment matures.

Fixed-income investments (loans) are issued for a specified period of time. When the time is up, the loan is due. The amount that will be paid back is called the *face value* — $1,000 for a bond, $10,000 for a treasury bill, etc.

Some fixed-income investments have long maturities (ten to thirty years). These include government bonds, corporate bonds, and convertible debentures. Some others have intermediate maturities (one to ten years), like government notes and intermediate corporate bonds. Among those with short maturities (one week to one year) are CDs, treasury bills, bankers' acceptances, and commercial paper. The common denominators of all fixed-income investments are two: they have a fixed payout, and they will be redeemed at face value on the date of maturity.

Preferreds, Convertible Preferreds, and Convertible Debentures
People have been known to say, "If it walks like a duck and

quacks like a duck, it's a duck." But what if it walks like a duck and moos like a cow? What then? This is the dilemma of preferred, convertible preferred, and convertible debenture issues. These unique investments are all hybrids. Some people feel that since they pay a fixed interest, they should be considered as fixed-income investments. Others claim that because their price movements are more closely correlated with stocks, they should be considered as stocks.

Both types of thinking are correct. Or, more accurately, there is no definite answer. Preferred, convertible preferred, and convertible debentures are slightly less risky than common stocks, and slightly more risky than bonds. (Debentures are backed only by the credit of the issuing corporation. Convertible debentures may be exchanged for common or preferred stock of the same corporation.)

Short-Term Fixed-Income Investments

Short-term fixed-income investments are just what the term implies — fixed-income investments which are issued with short maturities. These maturities may range from one day to one year. Knowing the types of short-term investments available to you and their characteristics and conditions is important for executing the no-cost and low-cost strategies presented in Section IV.

Certificates of Deposit

Certificates of deposit (CDs) are, in effect, loans to the bank that issues them. The terms (or maturities) of these loans vary from three months to five years, but only those issued for one year or under are considered short-term investments.

CDs used to be illiquid, meaning you couldn't cash them in early without suffering a stiff penalty. Also, they were originally issued in minimum denominations of $10,000. But as competition for your dollars (deposits) increased, some banks created CDs with special features, such as smaller denominations, or the privilege of withdrawing a portion of the funds without penalty.

CDs are insured by the FDIC and FSLIC, just as savings and checking accounts are. But only the principal is insured, not the interest, and only up to $100,000. This $100,000 ceiling includes other accounts you may have under any one name.

Recently, certain large brokerage firms have opened funds that make CDs available in units of $1,000. Brokerage firms can buy thousands or tens of thousands of CDs from banks. (1,000 CDs = $1,000,000.) Therefore, they may get better (higher) rates than you, the average investor, can obtain. They can then pool these CDs and offer units of $1,000 denominations to their clients. This alternative may be the right one for you, since the risk is minimized because the CDs offered by a broker represent diversified holdings of several banks' CDs. And you need not make the often prohibitive commitment of $10,000. Again I suggest some shopping around, as the rates do vary.

Commercial Paper

Commercial paper is short-term paper issued by a corporation. The minimum unit is $100,000. Generally this instrument affords liquidity (since it may be traded before maturity) and higher interest rates than treasury bills or certificates of deposit. Most of us cannot afford to buy commercial paper directly, but since commercial paper is a large portion of the holdings of money market mutual funds, you can get the benefit of the higher rate by investing in them instead.

Money Market Funds or Liquid Reserve Funds

Money market mutual funds are generally listed in a section of their own in the newspaper. The listings include the name of the fund manager as well as the name of the fund. (A particular manager may manage a number of different funds.) The listings also include the size of the fund's assets (in millions), the average maturity in days, the seven-day average yield in percent, and a thirty-day average yield in percent. The name of the fund is simply the sponsoring organization. The assets define the size of the fund;

they have no bearing whatsoever on either the return on the investment or the quality of the sponsoring organization. The average maturity tells you the average number of days it would take for the short-term investments in the fund to mature. When an investment comes due and the proceeds must be reinvested, we say the fund has "turned over." A fund that turns over in thirty days will have many new securities after the thirty days. The longer the fund takes to mature, the slower the yield changes. Conversely, the sooner the fund matures, the more quickly it adjusts to the daily interest rate changes. When interest rates are going up, the knowledgeable investor buys money market funds with a short maturity. When rates go down a fund with long-term maturity is best because they drop more slowly. But no one, not even a professional money manager, can predict accurately the direction or magnitude of interest rate changes. For this reason, a wise investor chooses a fund that offers a fairly high seven-day or thirty-day average yield. The yield on the fund changes from day to day, because each day some of the securities come due and are then reinvested at the current rate. The seven-day average yield reflects the average of the last seven days' yield on the fund, while the thirty-day average yield is the amount an investor would have earned, on average, for the previous thirty days. Currently the average maturity in days varies from one day to forty-one days. The seven-day average yield varies from 16.9 to 18.3, and the thirty-day average yield varies from 16.5 to 18.2

Bonds

Bond quotations appear in the financial section of the newspaper as follows:

Bonds	Current Yield	Sales in $1000	High	Low	Last	Net Change
ABC 15S91	15.9	88	95 7/8	95	95 1/8	− 5/8

ABC refers to the name of the company that issues the bond or debt. The coupon is 15 percent, which means that the holder of this bond will receive $150 (15 percent of the face value of $1,000) annually. Since the letter S appears after the 15, this $150 will be paid in two semiannual installments of $75 each. This particular bond will mature in 1991, and its current yield is 15.9 percent. On this one day, $88,000 worth of this bond were traded. Bonds are issued in units of $1,000, but are quoted in terms of $100. Therefore, to calculate the actual price of the bond, multiply the price quoted by 10; when a bond is quoted as 95-1/8, it sells for $951.25. The high of the day was 95-7/8 and the low was 95. The bond closed at 95-1/8 with a net change of − 5/8, which means the bond had closed the day before at 95-3/4. Which price is the most relevant?

They all are. They represent the range of prices at which the bond traded during that day; and if you wanted to buy the bond the next day, most likely you would offer the price quoted at the close.

Sometimes, however, there are "gap openings." If so, the next morning, when the exchange starts trading, the bond may open at a price significantly higher or lower than the previous day's close. This means that some vital information may have reached the marketplace after the exchanges closed. Such a piece of information may be a change in the money supply, an increase in the prime lending·rate, or new legislation that will affect the level of interest rates.

To further complicate matters, there are three different kinds of yield: coupon yield, current yield, and yield to maturity. To understand the bond market, you will need to become familiar with each of the three types.

To return to our example, the ABC Company's bond is "15 of 91." The 15 is the coupon, or interest, the company originally agreed to pay; in other words, the company guaranteed that it would pay $150 each year to the holder of each $1,000 bond. The "S" refers to the period of payment, which in this case is semi-annually. The bond may fluctuate in price up or down, but in either case the holder will continue to get $150 a year for each bond held regardless of the current price of the bond.

Assume for simplicity's sake that the bond was quoted at 95, which means it sold for $950. If an investor purchased a $1,000 bond for $950 and received $150 per year in interest from the company, the actual current yield would be 15.8 percent (150 divided by 950 equals .158). The investor would continue to earn this yield on the invested dollars as long as he held the bond. Had this bond on this particular day been quoted at $105, the current yield would have been approximately 14.3 percent.

The third kind of yield, called "yield to maturity," is somewhat more complex. Say that exactly one year before maturity you buy the same $1,000-face-value bond for $950. Assume that it is paying the same $150 per year. When the bond matures one year after the date of purchase, you will get back the full face amount of $1,000. That is $50 more than you paid. That $50 is considered a capital gain. You will also get the $150 in interest during the year you hold the bond. All in all, you will have received $200 for your investment of $950. But you didn't have the $50 to invest during the year. So your yield to maturity is just over 18 percent. If, though, you purchased the bond ten years before maturity rather than one year, as in the above-mentioned example, that $50 gain would have to be prorated over the ten years. Thus you would be getting $150 each year in interest plus an eventual extra $50 on maturity. This equals an extra $5, on average, each year, assuming you hold the bond until maturity. Your annual average yield to maturity would be approximately $155 each year, or 16.3 percent on your initial $950 investment.

If you had taken a calculator in hand, you would have noticed that these numbers appear wrong; after all, $200 divided by $950 is 21 percent, not 18 percent. The reason for the 18 percent yield to maturity involves the reinvestment period and the reinvestment rate on the dividends. You only have use of the dividend after it is paid: in the one-year example you have the first $75 only after six months, and the second $75 plus $50 appreciation only after one year.

Although the yield to maturity most accurately describes your actual returns, newspapers rarely quote it because it involves complex calculations and assumptions about the reinvestment rate that your dividends will earn during the holding period of the bond.

Why Do Bond Prices Fluctuate?

In the previous example, the ABC Company issued a 15 percent coupon bond because the prevailing interest rate for the company's quality rating and the bond's maturity was 15 percent at the time of issuance. Subsequent to when the bond was issued, the general level of interest rates has gone up, and therefore the bond's yield to maturity and current yield have gone up and its market price has declined, but its coupon (by definition) has remained the same, $150 per year. The bond issue now competes in the market alongside new issues of similar maturity, with coupons of about 18 percent. No one who can get 18 percent will accept a 15 percent yield for a similar bond. This reality forces down the bond's market price until the coupon ($150 a year) provides a yield that competes with current rates. To repeat: If you can invest $1,000 in an 18 percent bond, why pay $1,000 for a 15 percent bond? In the example of the ABC Company's bond, the price dropped from $1,000 to $950. Conversely, if prevailing interest rates had gone down, the value of the bond would have gone up because its yield would then compete with new bond issues offering lower current yields, making its high coupon more attractive to investors.

Interest Rates and Yield Curves

When the demand for loans exceeds the supply of available credit, the price of loans (the interest rate) goes up; when the supply of credit exceeds the demand for loans, the price of loans goes down. Expectations of higher or lower interest rates influence the direction of rates as well as the shape of the yield curve.

Yield curve. At any point in time, different interest rates prevail for different maturities. Historically, longer-term bonds have had higher yields, and shorter-term bonds or short-term paper have had lower yields. In order to buy bonds that mature in twenty or thirty years, investors have traditionally demanded higher interest rates to compensate for the higher risks.

To illustrate:

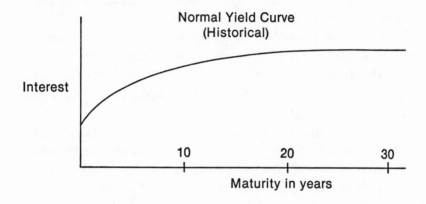

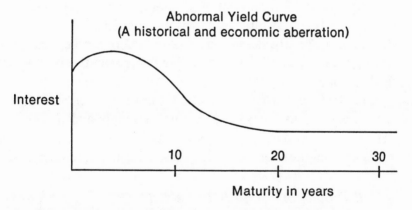

In the past few years the yield curve has been abnormal relative to historical norms resulting from pressures on the short-term money supply and apprehension about short-term economic prospects. Now rates are slowly coming back toward the traditional curve. This "realignment" has presented some interesting investment opportunities in the long end of the bond market (long maturities). By knowing the shape of the current yield curve, you may be able to make better decisions as to the optimum maturities of your fixed-income investments; it will help you decide whether you should stay in short maturities or lock in longer-term returns.

Quality

The quality of bonds ranges from very good to very poor — ratings made by such independent services as Moody's and Standard & Poor's, based on their judgments of the creditworthiness of the various credit obligations and the issuing companies. The ratings starting from the top are as follows: Aaa (Moody's) or AAA (Standard & Poor's), Aa or AA, A, Baa or BBB, Ba or BB, B, Caa or CCC, Ca or CC, C.

Quality ratings translate directly into bond prices and yields. A top-quality company is much less likely to experience financial difficulties that would prevent timely payment of interest and repayment of principal, and therefore its bond is a "safer" investment. As a result the investor will accept a lower interest rate or yield than on a bond of lesser quality. Companies or municipalities that only have a Baa or A rating must offer higher interest rates to compensate investors for the increased risk. In poor markets the prices of lower-quality bonds tend to decline faster than those of higher-quality bonds.

Sometimes, bonds of higher and lower quality sell at about the same yield because of special factors of supply and demand. In that case, it's always wise to buy the better quality, since the market is offering little or no compensation for taking higher risks.

Call Protection: Who Is Protected?

"Call provisions" give the issuer the right to redeem (buy back) the bonds prior to their maturity date under specified conditions. The call price is always at a premium over the face value of $1,000. For example, a corporation issues a thirty-year bond with a 15 percent coupon, with a five-year call protection. This bond is callable at $105 ($5 premium over par). Five years later interest rates drop to 12 percent. The corporation can now benefit by paying the additional cost involved in calling the bonds at $105 and floating another bond issue at 12 percent. Of course, you end up with a profit, but now your $1,050 can only be reinvested at 12 percent, and maybe you were counting on the 15 percent coupon. Call protection really protects the corporation against having to pay higher interest rates if general interest rates drop. It permits the corporation to recall an expensive loan in order to refinance it at a lower cost.

Types of Bonds

A *bearer bond* (or *coupon bond*) is one whose owner's name is not registered with the issuer. Thus in some ways it is equivalent to cash. A coupon (or piece of paper) is attached to the bond and serves as evidence that interest is payable to the presenter, usually once every six months. The coupon rate is the annual interest rate pledged by the issuer to the bondholder. The coupon amount is the dollar amount you will receive when this paper is submitted to a bank (or through your broker) for collection.

A *registered bond* is recalled in the name of the holder on the banks of either the issuer of the bond or the issuer's agent. The owner is mailed a check when the interest is due, and the bond can be transferred only if the certificate is endorsed.

Issuer Types

Besides differences in maturity, price, coupon, and quality, there are other differences — differences in the type of issuer and in the terms and conditions attached to the bonds. Here is a brief description of some of the various types of bonds.

Government and Agency Issues

1. Treasury bills (t-bills) — short-term marketable U.S. Treasury obligations with maturities ranging from ninety days to one year which are offered on a discount basis. A one-year $10,000 t-bill with a 15 percent yield can be bought at approximately $8,500. When the year is up, you receive the full $10,000. The

minimum denomination is $10,000. T-bills can be sold through a broker at a price that includes the interest accrued to the point of sale.

2. U.S. treasury notes — securities with maturities of one to ten years. These may carry specialized coupons.

3. U.S. treasury bonds — obligations maturing in more than ten years. Many treasury bonds outstanding today were sold many years ago at much lower prevailing interest rates. Because of their comparatively low coupon — 3 to 7 percent — they sell at deep discounts from par value. Long-term treasury bonds issued in recent years may carry coupons of 15 percent or higher.

4. Federal agency issues — securities issued by federal agencies created by Congress over a long span of years and ranking in caliber just below U.S. government securities.

5. Mortgage pass-through certificates — a certificate of participation in a pool of mortgages that a mortgage-lending institution has sold to a trustee. Investors in pass-through certificates receive monthly payments of interest and principal as the mortgages in the pool are paid off.

Corporate Bonds

1. First-mortgage bond — a corporate bond secured by a mortgage on all or part of the fixed property of the issuing corporation.

2. Debenture — a corporate bond backed only by the general credit of the issuing corporation and not by any pledge of property.

3. Convertible debenture — a bond issued on the general credit of the corporation which may be converted into common stock and sometimes preferred stock of the same corporation at a specified price under stated conditions.

Mortgage-Backed Bonds

Mortgage-backed bonds are issued by a bank or institution which lends mortgage money to homeowners. They have as collateral a sizable amount of mortgages — usually a larger dollar amount than the total dollar amount of the available bonds.

Municipal Bonds

Municipal bonds are obligations issued by a city, town, village, state, territory, or U.S. possession. All these bonds are exempt from federal income taxes but are sometimes subject to state and city taxes, especially if the municipal bond is issued in a state different from the bondholder's resident state.

The worksheet on page 110 will help you to inventory your own current bond holdings. (There is another table for short-term fixed income on page 161 in Section IV under "No-Risk Strategies.")

In addition to taking inventory, you may want to keep a record of interesting potential investments. For that purpose we have supplied also a potential bond investment worksheet (page 111).

Finding a Broker

Although it is possible to buy CDs and t-bills through a local bank, in order to buy and sell securities (stocks, bonds, options) you will need a broker. Don't be put off by the stereotypical brokers you've seen on television. Although they deal in millions of dollars' worth of securities per half-hour segment, most real brokers are very happy to take on clients who have modest sums to invest. What's more, the right broker can help you to expand your financial know-how, thus giving you more command of your investment decisions.

In a sense, it's quite easy to find a broker; all you have to do is look in the telephone book under "Stock and Bond Brokers." But

BOND INVENTORY WORKSHEET

(1) Name, Coupon and Maturity	(2) Quality	(3) Number of Bonds	(4) Current Yield	(5) Current Price	(6) Current Value $
Corporates					
Example:					
ABC, 15's 91	AA	5	13.2%	$91	$4550
___	___	___	___	___	___
___	___	___	___	___	___
___	___	___	___	___	___
Government					
___	___	___	___	___	___
___	___	___	___	___	___
___	___	___	___	___	___
___	___	___	___	___	___
Agencies (Pass-Through, Mortgage-Backed and Straight Agencies)					
___	___	___	___	___	___
___	___	___	___	___	___
___	___	___	___	___	___
Municipals (Tax-Exempt)					
___	___	___	___	___	___
___	___	___	___	___	___
___	___	___	___	___	___

Column (1): Name of issuer, coupon, and the year of maturity.
(2): Quality rating of the bond. In some cases the quality rating of a particular bond is lower than the rating of its issuer. This difference may be accounted for by the quality of the backing (first-mortgage bonds and revenue bonds) or the lack thereof.
(3): Number of bonds — number of bonds purchased or size of the lot.
(4): Current yield = coupon ÷ current price.
(5): Current price may be obtained from the newspaper or your broker.
(6): Current value = number of bonds × current price.

POTENTIAL BOND INVESTMENT WORKSHEET

(1) Name, Coupon and Maturity	(2) Quality	(3) Number of Bonds	(4) Current Yield	(5) Current Price	(6) Current Value $
Corporates					
Example:					
ABC, 15's 91	AA	5	13.2%	$91	$4550
___	___	___	___	___	___
___	___	___	___	___	___
___	___	___	___	___	___
Government					
___		___	___	___	___
___		___	___	___	___
___		___	___	___	___
___		___	___	___	___
Agencies (Pass-Through, Mortgage-Backed and Straight Agencies)					
___	___	___	___	___	___
___	___	___	___	___	___
___	___	___	___	___	___
Municipals (Tax-Exempt)					
___	___	___	___	___	___
___	___	___	___	___	___
___	___	___	___	___	___

Column (1): Name of issuer, coupon, and the year of maturity.
    (2): Quality rating of the bond. In some cases the quality rating of a particular bond is lower than the rating of its issuer. This difference may be accounted for by the quality of the backing (first-mortgage bonds and revenue bonds) or the lack thereof.
    (3): Number of bonds — number of bonds purchased or size of the lot.
    (4): Current yield = coupon ÷ current price.
    (5): Current price may be obtained from the newspaper or your broker.
    (6): Current value = number of bonds × current price × 10.

that's not a terribly good way to go about it. Start out by checking with friends and relatives whose judgment you trust, because it is useful to have personal impressions. Be sure that whomever you talk with has actually dealt with the broker personally; no one can judge a broker's competence from hearsay. Another good reason to use a broker who has the accounts of friends and/or relatives is the leverage you get. He knows that neglecting your needs or taking inappropriate action with your account could negatively affect the other relationships he has built up. It may be in your best interest that the broker you choose should work for a firm affiliated with the New York Stock Exchange, but it is not essential that the firm be in your own town or city, because you can do business by phone or by mail with a company somewhere else. Most cities or towns do however have at least one brokerage house.

There are two kinds of brokerage firms, *full service* and *discount,* and each serves a different kind of investor.

Full-Service Brokers

If you know little about investments or you are looking for investment advice, you would be better off doing business with a large national or regional full-service firm. The big firms generally have competent research departments and also offer a variety of products. They also provide special services to small investors — services like research reports, investment leads, tax shelters, mutual funds, limited partnerships.

Full-service firms provide a one-step way of investing, and that is their main advantage. The disadvantage is that, like the members of any other profession, stockbrokers display varying levels of ability: some have very good ideas of their own; others parrot what they hear from colleagues. Some know when the market is in trouble; others insist (and perhaps believe) that everything is fine even when the market is falling apart. Some give you advice about when to sell a stock, as well as when to buy; others forget about the stock once you've bought it. For these reasons, you have to work with brokers for a while to learn how they serve their clients.

That is why you should seek out personal recommendations before choosing a broker.

Market outlooks, earnings and price projections on specific companies, and industry analyses are some of the reports available through a full-service brokerage firm. But there is a lot of additional information you may want: historical earnings, price ranges, quality ratings, sources of earnings, holdings of a mutual fund, etc. This information may be available at both types of firms. Don't feel embarrassed to ask. It could save you a lot of homework.

Discount Brokers

Discount brokerage firms are for people who are capable of managing their own investments; for people who get advice from paid advisers other than brokers; and for people who have large orders to place. The larger the order, the larger the discount. So if you have your own investment ideas and simply need to get your orders executed, or if you want to sell some stocks from an inheritance, a discount broker may be the right one for you. A discount firm offers no advisory services. No networks of salespeople. No long discussions on investment alternatives. No research services to speak of. Discount brokers just take orders; you tell them what you want to buy or sell, and they carry out your instructions. On smaller trades, the commission generally runs 20 to 25 percent lower than that charged by a full-service brokerage firm. On larger trades, the savings can be as high as 70 to 80 percent.

Discount brokers do deal in such extras as margin accounts, money market funds, options, pricing, and low commission rates. In fact they offer many of the services that full-service firms offer. Their low commission rates are possible because, as mentioned, they do not have to bear the cost of staffing a research department (security analysts are very highly paid), and in many instances their brokers are salaried, so the firm saves the commission they would be paying on every trade.

One further point: all discount brokerage firms belong to the

Securities Investors Protection Corporation (SIPC), which insures individual accounts for up to $100,000, so your investment has the same protection it would have in a full-service brokerage firm.

What to Expect from Your Broker

Be candid with your broker. Tell him or her about your investment goals; no broker, however talented, can serve you well without knowing what you want. But never feel committed to following his advice; he works to serve you, not the other way around. Some investors even work with several brokers simultaneously, so they can get a variety of opinions. Whether you work with one or several is your own business, but you have the right to expect that your broker or brokers will give you honest, reliable service, as well as realistic information about the current state of the market; that they understand your investment goals and expectations; and that they exercise good judgment.

Reading the Fine Print

Brokers are not really salesmen for the companies whose stocks they sell; they are salesmen for their brokerage firms and, above all, for themselves. And their advice can be as self-interested as that of any other salesman. A dear friend of mine whom I'll call Laura found this out the hard way.

In a career that spanned more than twenty years, Laura had managed to put away a small nest egg. Her investments were, as they should have been, rather conservative: a few AAA bonds, a few utility stocks, and a money market account. One day Laura was told by her friend Jim that he had made a bundle through a broker who traded stock options. Laura was excited. Jim arranged for her to meet the broker, who one evening came to her house with an array of charts, brochures, and forms. He claimed that his strategies were very safe, and he even tried to explain them; but Laura told him, "Never mind. I don't really understand what you're saying. But if it works, go ahead and do it."

The broker stopped his sales pitch and told her that she would have to sign forms — "Just so that I can do my job properly," he added. Laura signed, but she did not read what she was signing. As it turned out, one form was a "discretionary agreement," which allows a broker to invest and trade the client's assets without first notifying the client. The "options agreement" that she signed allowed the broker to trade options or puts and calls. Finally, she signed an agreement for a "margin account," which pledges her stocks and bonds as collateral so the broker can buy on margin. The collateral covers any losses that may occur. When Laura signed this form, she pledged the entire value of her investment portfolio as security for the purchase of options. Her existing conservative assets would have to cover any losses that might occur as a result of these options transactions.

Laura began to get monthly statements from the brokerage firm — a very large, well-known and respected one. To Laura, these statements looked complicated. And they are; you need practice to interpret them accurately. In addition to the monthly statements, Laura began to get checks in different amounts in different months — $200, $300, $400. This made her think she was making a profit.

The broker eventually left the firm, and Laura decided to take her account to another brokerage house. Her new broker called a week after the transfer and asked her if she knew that she had had a debit balance in her previous account.

"Debit?" Laura stammered. "Impossible. I've been making money all along."

"No," he insisted, "you owed $18,000, and we've already paid that off."

After looking through Laura's statements, I learned that the checks she had received were simply the dividends and interest she had earned on her conservative stocks and bonds.

Laura had no idea that, by signing the margin agreement, she had in essence pledged her entire portfolio. And the losses had at one point been as high as $38,000 — a fact she of course had never even suspected. What about the broker? He became rich from all the commissions he earned. Was it legal? Alas, yes. Laura signed willingly. Ethical? Heavens, no. It is one of the most unethical practices I have heard of. But it happens every day.

Had Laura understood the risk inherent in trading options, had she asked about the margin account, had she understood what discretionary powers are, she would not have signed any of the forms. She learned her lesson well, so well that now she will not buy her monthly commutation ticket without first reading it. Sure, it's embarrassing to ask questions that may make you seem ignorant. Forget the embarrassment; nobody ever died of it. Ask questions until you understand every word, phrase, provision, and comma in anything you sign. You will regret it someday if you do not.

Summary

Here are some questions to ask yourself or your potential broker before making a decision:

Full-Service

1. Did the broker ask about your investment goals, your current financial situation, your risk tolerance, your tax bracket, your other assets or other sources of income?

2. Is the broker currently working with people in circumstances similar to yours?

3. Are the broker's other clients pleased with the service and performance they have gotten?

4. Does the firm have the capability to invest your "loose" cash (from interest, dividends, or proceeds of sales) in a quick and efficient manner? Sending you a check once a month does not necessarily constitute "quick" or "efficient" service.

5. When is this broker likely to issue a "sell" recommendation?

6. What is the track record of the recommendations of the research department?

Discount Brokerage Firms

1. Who executes the trades? Do they have their own "floor" brokers? (Floor brokers are on the floor of the exchange and actually execute the trades. The broker on the phone simply takes your order and transmits it to the floor broker.)

2. Can the firm invest your "loose" cash (from interest, dividends, or proceeds of sales) quickly and efficiently?

3. If you'd like to trade options, do they have a competent options trader? On which exchange or exchanges?

4. What information is contained in your monthly statement?

5. Does the broker have access to Moody's bond ratings, Standard & Poor's stock reports and mutual funds reports, or Value Line services? (Value Line services are publications which provide ratings, financial histories and/or earnings estimates for stocks and bonds.)

Collectibles

The nineteen-seventies saw a boom in the price of collectibles, a catchall word referring in general terms to art, antiques, precious gemstones, stamps, coins, rare books, vintage cars, and other items too numerous to mention. The uncertain economy of the early seventies, along with rising inflation, made the more traditional investments such as stocks and bonds seem less attractive. Stories began to appear in newspapers and magazines about collections — antique brass, ivory carvings, Shirley Temple spoons — that, begun as a hobby, had turned into investments of intrinsic value.

Cocktail party talk is studded with stories about somebody's brother-in-law who bought something for 25 cents at a yard sale and subsequently sold the item for $80. The owner had no idea that the 25-cent investment was worth anything. And this very fact is one of the disadvantages of collectibles.

The market for collectibles tends toward illiquidity, which makes it difficult to get an accurate quote on the worth of an item at any one time. And even if you can get a quote, it may be difficult to sell the item at that price quickly. For every story of a gem found in the junkpile, there is one about an investor who paid $125 for an item and was obliged to sell it, when the time came, for $50 — whatever the traffic would bear.

As with any boom, there is good news and bad news. The good news is that since more people are into collectibles, some of these vehicles have become more liquid. The bad news is that there are many unscrupulous entrepreneurs waiting to take advantage of the novice. There is a glut of unsound investments.

A variety of organizations are offering limited-edition books, coins, prints, silver ingots, and plates. The items are just that — limited editions: no more. There is no assurance that the value assigned or the price charged or the hint of appreciation has any basis in reality.

Anyone wanting to invest in collectibles must always be aware of the dangers as well as the advantages of this vehicle. The two most common dangers are fraud, where an item is represented as something that it is not; and overvaluation, where the price is way over and above what one could realize at resale.

We have all seen slick ads and many of us have received slick brochures touting some collectible item as "The Hedge Against Inflation." Gemstones, particularly diamonds, and art are two popular items urged on investors. The advertising material offers examples to prove that diamonds have doubled in value over a period of time or that certain art pieces are selling for ten times their original purchase price. These examples may be quite legitimate, but the potential investor is given very little pertinent information.

There are, for instance, over two thousand separate categories of diamonds. The overwhelming majority, 99 percent, have shown gains of less than 15 percent a year. Only the remaining top 1 percent of quality-grade stones have appreciated at faster rates. What is more — and this is where the element of fraud comes in — many firms claiming to sell high-quality gemstones are actually selling inferior stones. And unfortunately the average investor looking for an inflation hedge would not know a top-grade diamond from a piece of glass.

The same holds true for art. Certain pieces have appreciated substantially in value over the recent past. But again, unless one is an expert in art, there is the risk of forgery. Or the investor may be taken in by auction fever, which occurs when a group of prospective buyers are so stimulated by the sale — and a good auctioneer will see to that — that they bid up the prices of a piece beyond reason. There is, moreover, no guarantee that the purchaser would realize a profit if he were to reauction the piece. In fact, it is quite possible he would sustain a loss.

Another risk with collectibles is perishability. Items such as stamps, coins, vintage cars, rare books, and art may be lost in a fire or be damaged in some way that destroys their value. For this reason, anyone involved in buying collectibles should either arrange to store them in a safe place or carry full insurance on the items. The very wisest of investors do both. And bear in mind that insurance and storage costs can, and often do, add substantially to the cost of the investment.

The ones who make the really big profits in collectibles are not the investors so much as the dealers, who buy at wholesale and sell at retail — a markup ranging anywhere from 25 to 100 percent.

Here is an example, using diamonds again, of the risk of illiquidity inherent in this situation. An investor goes to a legitimate dealer and buys a top-grade diamond for $1,000. The stone is appraised and certified as top grade. However, when the investor returns to the same dealer to sell the diamond back, the dealer, no matter how reputable, may pay only $500, the wholesale price, to buy it back. For the investor to make a profit on this transaction, the stone would have had to more than double in value in the interim so that it would now be worth more than $1,000 wholesale.

In spite of all the pitfalls, any investor who is mindful of the dangers and disadvantages of collectibles can reap many substantial rewards. One is the simple joy and pleasure that comes from indulging in a fascinating hobby, and many collectibles are, indeed, fascinating subjects. The other is, frankly, financial. Many collectibles have undergone considerable price appreciation and have actually become inflation hedges.

Caveat Emptor

Each of us gets financial advice from many sources — from newspapers and television, from salesmen, from our in-laws. Most of us can tell when we're being given advice that is uninformed or uninspired. But not everybody can recognize advice that is self-interested. And much advice is. That's why in making investments and "buying" money, as in buying anything else, *caveat emptor* — "let the buyer beware."

Several months ago, I got a flyer in the mail for a seminar to be held at a well-known New York hotel. A "recognized" financial expert would discuss the current financial picture and also suggest inflation-beating investments for the future. I decided to attend the seminar, knowing well that the brochure I had received was probably exaggerated; but I was curious, so I sent in the registration form and in due time arrived at the hotel's conference room at the stated time. A pleasant young woman greeted me at the door and gave me a name tag and a portfolio of colorful folders. She urged me to have a cup of coffee and a doughnut while we waited for the seminar to begin.

At 9:30 A.M. an impeccably dressed, good-looking fellow in his mid-thirties entered the room. I didn't know whether to be more impressed by his fine speaking voice or by the confidence he exuded. His entire manner was positive, and he held our attention by giving the impression that he knew a lot about the American economy. At first he seemed to know what he was talking about. But as I listened, I began to find many of his statements rather shallow. It seemed as though someone had briefed him well but that he himself did not really know a great deal — not enough to answer an in-depth question, for example. About forty-five minutes into his talk, which he illustrated with graphs, tables, and charts from an overhead projector, he came at last to the point.

The investments of the future, he announced in a tone that hinted darkly of revelation, were precious gemstones in general, and diamonds in particular. His message then became ever so simple and clear: to protect your money over the long haul, buy diamonds, and lots of them — big stones, little stones, round stones, square stones — any size or shape, as long as they were of the highest quality.

Some people in the audience seemed to be impressed. They nodded their heads ever so slightly and moved forward on their seats. The lecturer had total eye contact. I suspected a fair number of them were "converted"; they would buy the diamonds. As for me — well, I was keeping an open mind. Maybe he was right. I really don't know much about diamonds, except a few basics. I know that there are distinct disadvantages to investing in or owning diamonds: they do not earn interest; they must be stored in a safe place; they have to be insured for their full replacement value; and they are illiquid. These extra factors drive up the actual cost of the investment, in some cases substantially. Besides, I don't care for diamonds; and, for that matter, I do not enjoy owning diamonds. I do not enjoy wearing them. And I certainly would not walk the streets of any big city wearing a diamond.

Moreover, you cannot walk into a bank and cash in your diamonds. You cannot call a broker and say, "Sell my diamonds," as you can say, "Sell my ABC Company stock." To sell gemstones, you have to find a suitable buyer. The seller often has to pay the costs of appraisal and certification: another expense. Furthermore, if you sell your gems to a dealer, you will only get the wholesale or dealer prices, even though you had to pay for them at retail. The difference between the wholesale and retail prices can be as much as 25 to 100 percent. That's a big handicap to overcome.

Anyway, the lecturer finally came to the point in his spiel: "I can get you diamonds — wholesale." He then announced a break for refreshments. "If anyone has any questions," he urged, "ask them and I'll answer." Most of the audience rushed up and crowded around him. I went off into a corner and poured myself a cup of coffee and began to go through the brochures more carefully. From the second page I learned that the lecturer was a salesman for the company that sponsored the seminar. The promotional brochure did say he was a "recognized financial expert." What it did not say was, recognized by whom, and who considers him an expert. And this company — surprise! surprise! — was in the business of selling diamonds. In other words, every time anyone said to him, "Yes sir, I'm going to invest in diamonds," this fellow made a commission — his bread and butter. Naturally he was going to claim that diamonds were the best possible investment. Most salesmen will tell you that whatever they are selling is the best thing you can buy. Mutual funds salesmen will assure you that their funds are the best. Insurance salesmen will say their rates and their policies are the best. Just remember that the more you buy, the more money the salesmen make.

This is not to say that you cannot get good advice from salesmen; often you can. A salesman's reputation depends on his ability to give good, reliable advice. Salesmen who give their customers the feeling that they have been cheated do not prosper. But that does not mean that salesmen give you the best advice for your particular circumstances. Or that salesmen give you wholly unbiased advice. Or that salesmen will cut their own throats by telling you not to buy what they sell. Therefore a salesman who would like to maintain a long-term relationship may be more likely to give appropriate advice than the one who is going for that "one-time" deal — assuming, of course, that he knows his field and has superior products to offer.

So before buying or signing on the dotted line, ask yourself questions like, "Is this individual in a position to be neutral and unbiased?" "If I reject his advice, will this fellow still earn money?" "If he does make money, do I fare at least as well as he does?" If the answer to any of these questions is "No," stop and reconsider the source of the advice before you take it.

SECTION IV
INVESTMENT STRATEGIES

N

ow you know how much you are worth and how much you have available to invest. You know where to get additional funds and how to get hold of them. You know how much risk you can afford to take, financially and emotionally. And you've learned how investments behave. Now let's put all the information you have gathered to work for you. This is the *action* section, the strategy section — the part of the book that will enable you to decrease your liabilities, add to your assets, and increase your net worth.

The strategies are divided into five parts:

1. Cost-saving strategies
2. No-risk strategies
3. Low- to medium-risk strategies
4. Inflation hedges
5. High-risk strategies

Cost-saving strategies are designed to cut your cost of living without changing your life-style. They will help you to manage or decrease your expensive liabilities. The remaining strategies are devoted to increasing the value of your assets and should be used with respect to your personal and financial risk tolerance.

Cost Savings

Most of us tend to be rather careful with our purchases. When we shop for food we look for coupons or weekly specials. We wait for sales to buy clothes. We may even spend weeks shopping around for a new car. Yet very few of us ever give serious thought to other forms of cost savings, savings that can mean thousands of dollars, not just $20 or $500. No book in the world could deal with every possible small economy, since the weight of such a volume alone would make it rather difficult to carry it home from the store. So we'll concentrate on the larger economies — those that can save you thousands of dollars.

"Net net bottom line," all cost savings come in one of two ways. One is to reduce the amount of money you must pay to others. When you find a way to pay out less for your mortgage, your utilities, your taxes, college tuition, insurance, and interest on loans, you effect a cost saving.

The other way is to use money that is available to you, rather than your own money. You effect this type of cost saving every time you use someone else's money that is earmarked for you, as when you win a scholarship or receive a grant.

College Education

The cost of a college education is rising every year, as many of us well know. It now costs more than $10,000 a year to attend the average private four-year college. Sure, you might be able to pay for your children's college education or your own by saving and scrimping and putting away money year by year. But you can also get the money with fewer sacrifices. Keep in mind that every scholarship, every grant, and every low-cost loan you can get reduces that awesome cost of $40,000 for an undergraduate degree, leaving that much of your hard-earned money for you.

Did you know that, last year, 43 percent of all available scholarships in the U.S. went unused? They went unused because people did not know about them and thus did not apply for them. I understand all too well why people know nothing about this money; I never knew myself until one afternoon about eighteen years ago, early in my tenth grade. On that day my parents said to me, "Susie, we — ahem — are afraid we won't be able to put together enough money to send you to college, and that means you're going to have to do it on your own. Particularly if you want to go to the school of your choice."

This announcement was a bit disconcerting for me at the time, but it forced me to plan ahead, and in a big way. For the next two years I tried much harder to get high marks. In the eleventh grade I went to my high school counselor and explained the situation to him. "Let's get to work," he said. "You have a good record, and there should be a number of available scholarships."

During the next year I took every eligibility test I could find. One test was used by about 200 scholarships, since small organizations often try to save time and money by pooling their resources and using one test. I studied the list and asked my guidance counselor which of the scholarships I should apply for. It was just a question of checking boxes, you see. He answered, "Well, it's a #2 pencil, which is rather cheap — why don't you check all of them?" As a result of that one test, I got seven checks, totaling $2,800. Before applying, I had never even heard of four of the donor organizations.

There is an additional source that most people don't even bother to check: the company they themselves work for. My father and I made a few phone calls and discovered that his company offered two four-year scholarships of $2,000 per year. It was quite a large company, and all the many children of its employees were eligible. But only three employees had bothered to apply. In that rarefied atmosphere of limited competition, it was quite easy to get the scholarship.

Besides the seven scholarships I won through the exam and the scholarship I got from my father's employer, I also got a scholarship from the college I finally chose to attend. Their financial-need/scholastic-record scholarship brought in an additional $1,000 a year. A New York State regents scholarship added another $1,200 a year. And, by the way, New York is not the only state that offers scholarships — nearly all the fifty states award them. These state scholarships are given in the form of outright grants, or by a reduction in tuition at a state or local college or university. Ask your high school guidance counselor for more information.

To make up the difference between my scholarships and the total cost of room and board, I took out a government loan. At that time, government loans were available at 3 percent interest, repayable starting one year after graduation. I borrowed an amount greater than I immediately needed. I took the extra money and put it in a California savings bank that was paying 5 percent and used the interest income to supplement my living expenses. In addition, I worked throughout each summer and part-time during the school year to earn spending money. I went to college wholly on my own resources and other people's money. My parents never had to contribute a dime.

You may think that in order to qualify for a scholarship you have to be either brilliant or financially destitute. Not so . . . . More than 80,000 private scholarship funds whose requirements are neither financial nor academic exist in the United States. Many of these funds were created in memory of a child who was not able to complete college or who died young. Others are bequests, or scholarship trusts. Often the criteria for eligibility reflect the traits or interests of the person whose memory the fund honors. Or the scholarship fund may require the applicants to be musically gifted, interested in ecology, able to write well, inclined toward engineering, or blue-eyed with black hair. There is a group supporting almost every cause, interest, and specialty.

How do you locate scholarships? Your school guidance counselor is always the best starting point. Your library is the second source, for many books list foundations and other sources of scholarships, along with their eligibility requirements. In addition, a few commercial enterprises have computerized thousands upon thousands of scholarship sources. You just pay $25 to $100, fill out a single form, and you receive a list of scholarships you may be eligible for. Avoid using any of these agencies unless they guarantee a refund if they cannot locate any scholarship sources for you.

After you have checked out these general sources of information, make inquiries of all groups, organizations and institutions with which you have an affiliation that may offer scholarships. If you belong to a church, religious group, social organization, union, club, or veterans' organization, ask whether they offer scholarships and how to apply.

The U.S. military offers a number of ways of providing financial aid, such as ROTC. But in most cases those who accept the aid must agree to serve for a time in the U.S. armed forces.

As for colleges and universities, most of them have funds available for a number of different purposes — scholastic scholarships, financial-need scholarships, and sports scholarships, among other kinds — so check with the school that accepts you or your child.

And then, of course, there is Uncle Sam. The government has a number of programs, including low cost loans, grants that are interest-free and others that are completely free; i.e., that don't have to be paid back at all.

Government Grants and Loans

Nearly every American knows that the U.S. government underwrites a tuition assistance program. Few, however, realize that Uncle Sam offers a selection of outright grants to students, based on need or merit or both. The Pell Grant, to name one, is awarded annually on the basis of need. A student from a low-income family (the definition of low-income changes annually) can receive as much as $1,650 a year; the average award runs to about $900. Whatever the amount of the grant, the money is free and clear. There are no taxes to pay, no interest to pay, and certainly no principal to repay. While a Pell Grant cannot cover a year's tuition, it can certainly help. And of course no student is restricted to just one grant or scholarship. There are many, many more.

The best-known and most popular sources of government aid to education are the guaranteed loan programs. Under these programs, the bank charges the going interest rate, the borrower pays a lower rate, and the U.S. government picks up the difference. Uncle Sam also guarantees the loan against default.

On October 1, 1981, the regulations controlling government aid to education changed greatly. The greatest changes were made in the oldest program, guaranteed student loans. Congress raised the interest rate that the borrowers pay from 9 to 14 percent. It also imposed a 5 percent "origination fee," which means that a student who borrows $2,000 for tuition receives only $1,900. The other $100 is the origination fee which the government will use to support the program. Interest, however, is charged on the full $2,000. Repayment of the loan does not begin until six months after the student's schooling ends.

The third major change involves eligibility requirements, determined by adjusted gross income (Line 31 of Form 1040 or Line 11 of Form 1040A). Students from families with an adjusted gross income of $30,000 or less can borrow as much as $2,500 a year. Students whose families have a higher adjusted gross income may still be eligible for loans if they can demonstrate need. At present, need is calculated by adding together all monies available to the student. This includes scholarships, grants, other loans, and expected parental contribution. All families with adjusted gross incomes of more than $30,000 are expected to contribute to the cost of their children's education. The amount varies with income. A family with an adjusted gross income of $31,000 is expected to contribute $2,690. A family with an adjusted gross income of $60,000 is expected to contribute $9,000. The total of all money available to the student is then subtracted from the amount of the annual tuition. The difference between the two determines need. To qualify, the student must show a difference of at least $1,000.

To illustrate this point, let's look at two families, the Bakers and the Fletchers. Each family has an adjusted gross income of $34,000, which is over the automatic eligibility limit. The Bakers have a son enrolled in a university where the tuition is $3,500 a year. The Fletchers have a daughter enrolled in a university where the annual tuition is $6,500. Neither the Bakers' son nor the Fletchers' daughter receives any financial assistance from any other source except their parents. Yet one family can demonstrate need; the other cannot.

In each case, the expected parental contribution of $2,690 must be subtracted from the tuition.

Bakers	Fletchers
$3,500	$6,500
−2,690	−2,690
$ 810	$3,810

The Bakers are not eligible because the difference between the tuition and the parental contribution falls below the $1,000 minimum. The Fletchers, however, are eligible to borrow the maximum, $2,500.

The method of determining need, you will notice, favors those families paying higher tuition, and higher costs are usually associated with private colleges and universities. This means that more families can now consider sending their sons and daughters to the more prestigious schools, because the high costs of those schools, paradoxically, may reduce a family's burdens.

The chart on page 132 (dated August 1981) further clarifies the criteria for eligibility for federally guaranteed student loans. These criteria are a function of

a. type of school
b. number of children presently enrolled in a college or university.

Another popular program, auxiliary loans to assist students, allows the applicant's parents to borrow as much as $3,000 a year without regard to income. However, repayment of loans taken out under this program begins sixty days after the loan date. Like guaranteed student loans, auxiliary loans to assist students currently charge interest rates of 14 percent.

While the interest on both these loan programs has recently gone up more than 33 percent, the cost is still modest compared to a conventional loan. The interest, of course, remains tax deductible.

With so much scholarship money and so many loans available for academic purposes, do you really have to put money aside each month to ensure that your children will go to college? Perhaps. But perhaps not. In many cases, the best way is not to start saving early, but to start planning early. Planning could be worth as much as $40,000 for each child — maybe more in the future. Remember, I didn't get all those scholarships purely on financial need and scholastic record. I got them in part because I *tried* to get them.

Eligibility for Federally Guaranteed Student Loans
(Maximum income levels qualifying for $1,000 to $2,500)

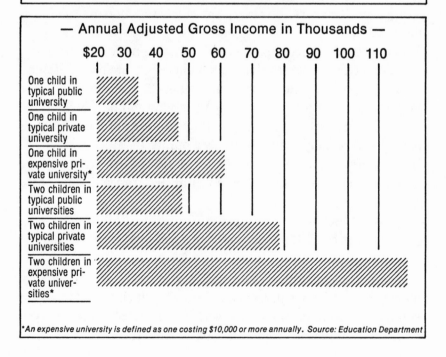

*An expensive university is defined as one costing $10,000 or more annually. Source: Education Department

"Homemade" Bill Consolidation

Another way of cutting your costs is to create a homemade bill consolidation loan. Bill consolidation, debt pooling, and debt liquidation all mean the same thing: pooling your current debts and getting money from another source to pay them off. By so doing, you pay only one monthly sum to only one creditor.

We've all seen the man on television who claims, "If installment payments or overdue bills trouble you, we will consolidate all your bills with one low monthly payment which you can afford. In addition, we will give you a long time to pay back this loan." This man is in fact offering you a debt-pooling or bill-consolidation loan, though a very imprudent one. When money is easy to obtain, interest charges are always very high — as high as 30 to 45 percent a year. Rarely does the TV salesman mention the interest; the rate is buried in the advertisement, which instead entices you with small monthly payments that may seem to be affordable. Let's look at these facts a little more closely.

First, any money that is very easily available is likely to be far more expensive than money from relatives, credit unions, most banks, employers, or savings and loan associations. After all, even though *you* may be a good credit risk, many of the people who have access to this money are *not*. So the lender has to make up for the additional risks by charging everyone the high rates.

Besides, although the money is paid back over a "long period of time," generally at least three to five years, you pay interest on the amount outstanding during each and every year. Furthermore, in many cases the interest is charged not on the current outstanding amount, but on the initial amount of the loan. In effect, the lender charges you "double" interest; halfway through the term of the loan you may already have repaid half of the amount outstanding, but you will still be paying interest on the money you repaid. The costs can really add up. Let's see how these loans really work.

Say you have $1,000 in bills outstanding. You take a $1,000 bill-consolidation loan at 30 percent per year, repayable over a five-year period. The lender tells you, "We will help you get out of trouble. All your bills will be taken care of, and you will pay us a monthly installment of only $42." Sounds good? Not when you realize that over the five years you will be repaying $2,500, of which $1,500 will be interest ($300 a year for five years). In other words, you will have ended up paying interest charges of 150 percent. Remember, too, that most debt consolidators will charge you interest rates higher than 30 percent.

Another point to keep in mind is that sometimes these "bill consolidators" take the money but do not pay the bills they have agreed to pay. Many such cases are now pending in courts or being investigated by the Better Business Bureau.

Should anyone *ever* take out a bill-consolidation loan? The answer is "yes," but only when it is cheaper to do so than to continue to pay your bills in their present form. Creating such a homemade bill-consolidation loan begins with assessing the amount that you must borrow in order to consolidate your bills. Let's take the $1,000 example mentioned before. First, scan your list of borrowing sources to find out where you can get money at the lowest possible rate. Say that it is 12 percent from either a credit union, a pension fund, an employer, or friends and relatives.

If you borrow this $1,000 at 12 percent and pay it in monthly installments, with interest charged only on the outstanding balance, you can pay back the entire amount in two years; and, lo and behold, your monthly payment is still under $50. The total cost of this loan comes to about $180 over the two-year period, at which point the debt will be totally eliminated. In this case the "homemade" version can represent a cost savings to you of $1,320, as compared with the cost of the commercial bill-consolidation loan.

A further refinement of this cost-saving strategy is to divide your current debts into those on which interest is charged and those on which it is not. Doctor bills, dentists' bills, and utilities and telephone bills are not generally subject to interest charges, while interest on credit cards, installment loans, time purchases, and car loans is often expensive.

First, send a proposal, preferably in writing, to those creditors who do not charge interest, offering to pay off the debts over the next year in monthly payments. In most cases, the creditors will be willing to cooperate with you; it is very expensive for them to turn your account over to debt-collection services, which keep from 25 to 50 percent of the amount they collect.

Now find out how much interest you are paying on the other portion of your debt. Check to see if you can borrow money at interest rates below those you are currently paying. If you can — which will probably be the case — pool these debts and pay them off immediately with your homemade bill-consolidation loan. Suppose you owe $5,000, on which you are being charged an average interest of 22 percent (i.e., a $1,500 credit card debt at 18 percent, and a $3,500 balance on a car loan at 24 percent). Borrowing $5,000 at 12 percent to pay back these debts can save you over $600 per year, or even more if you pay back that $5,000 in installments.

A final note: in some cases, bank loans impose prepayment penalties, which means they charge you for paying loans back before maturity. To decide whether you can still save money, even after paying the penalty, determine the amount of interest you still owe and subtract that penalty. If that difference is positive, it still pays for you to do it. Even if you can easily afford the monthly payments on your loan, you will save money if you borrow the cheap money to pay off the expensive money.

What if you don't have access to any cheap money and your bills are piling up? What should you do now?

First, what *not* to do:

1. Don't take out a commercial bill-consolidation loan.

2. Don't declare bankruptcy.

Personal bankruptcies are to be resorted to only in the most extreme cases because they carry some very serious stigmas.

As a result of rising costs, rising inflation, rising interest rates, and advertising by lawyers, the number of personal bankruptcies has more than quadrupled in the last five years. In every case of bankruptcy, your creditors lose out. All your past debts are wiped out, and you are left with enough to start over again. Sounds good, right? WRONG. In the past, prospective creditors might have said, "This person owes nothing; therefore, he is a good credit risk."

Today, however, creditors fear that consumers see bankruptcy as an "easy way out." They say: "This person squirmed out of his obligations last time; he may do so again." In addition to this, a personal bankruptcy stays on your credit history for ten years! What will you do when you need a new house? a new car? an installment loan? or a credit card?

But what *should* you do if you can't pay your bills? You should do exactly what you did for the non-interest-bearing bills in the last section: Calculate what you can afford to pay off over the next year and try to get your creditors to agree to your proposal. Then follow up with a letter confirming whatever agreement you have reached. Say you owe the electric utility company $120. Offer to pay $10 extra each month for a year. As we've said, in most cases the company will cooperate, since it is very expensive for them to collect through a collection agency.

If your creditors are uncooperative, get in touch with your local consumer credit counseling service. Most major cities have them, and their services are free to you, the consumer. Consumer credit counseling services (also known as credit counseling services) are supported by contributions from large corporations who find them a viable alternative to collection agencies.

These counseling services will themselves contact your creditors to help get you out of the hole.

Life Insurance

Esquire magazine's seventeenth rule of friendship is: "A friend will refrain from telling you he picked up the same amount of life insurance coverage you did for half the price and *his* is noncancelable."

Life insurance is one product that so many people pay so much for and know so little about. One reason is that the average consumer can read a utility bill far more easily than he can a life insurance policy. Yet, over a ten-year period, that average consumer will spend far more for life insurance than for electricity. In most cases he can justify his lack of knowledge with the excuse that life insurance is so complex, and, besides, it's easier simply to follow the advice of an insurance salesman. But the salesman's job is to convince you that you bought the "best" policy for the "best" price.

Insurance salesmen can serve as estate planners if they know their insurance products and are capable of helping you to work out a program. But remember, their advice is colored by self-interest. The main source of their income is the commissions they receive on the insurance they sell. Some agents are willing to search out the right kind of life insurance for your own personal needs, but others are content to work on the principle that any insurance leaves you better off than you would have been without it. Most of us are not knowledgeable enough to question life insurance salesmen and therefore cannot find out whether they are giving us accurate information. The apparent complexity works very much in the salesmen's favor. But just knowing the basic concepts behind life insurance and shopping around can help tremendously.

A recent study on life insurance premiums showed that the cost for the same kind of life insurance policy can be as much as four times higher at one source than another. Remember, the job of the life insurance salesman or agent is not to make your decisions for you, but to help you buy the necessary amount of coverage at the best price.

Low-Cost Insurance
Group insurance. You purchase group insurance, not as an individual, but as a member of a group. In many cases, group in-

surance costs far, far less than do individual policies. Often, an employer may pay for a certain amount of insurance and give employees the option to buy additional amounts themselves. Since the rates are usually lower than you could get with individual coverage, it's smart to load up on all the employer insurance you can get. But what happens when you leave your job? Most group insurance can be converted to individual coverage within thirty days. The cost, however, may be quite high. If you are uninsured, or insurable only at high-risk rates, you may choose to convert. Otherwise, it pays to shop elsewhere for coverage at this point.

Teachers' unions, veterans' associations, and many other organizations also offer group coverage of all types for their members. Also, professional, fraternal, and alumni groups may arrange for their members to buy policies, sometimes at bargain rates. Whenever you want additional coverage or lose your employee insurance benefits, try to buy a policy from one of those sources.

Savings bank life insurance (SBLI). Savings bank life insurance is available in relatively few states, but those states are the populous ones, and the rates for SBLI are often the lowest. There is one drawback in all cases: there is an upper limit to the amount of coverage you can get from them. If SBLI is available to you, use it as your primary source of insurance and take out as much as you can.

State-sponsored insurance. Some states offer you straight-life or term insurance up to the age of sixty-five at very low cost, directly from the state. Get in touch with your state insurance commission to find out if your state provides insurance, and if it does, get as much as you can; the amount is always limited.

Credit unions. Many credit unions sell small amounts of life insurance to members who maintain savings accounts with them — perhaps $4,000 worth of insurance for $2,000 in savings. The amount may not be large, but with the exception of SBLI, life insurance from credit unions is the cheapest insurance around. An advantage to credit union insurance is the loan insurance they often offer to their creditors. If you have borrowed from your credit union and die before repaying the loan, this insurance pays the outstanding balance in full. This type of insurance may even be free to the borrower.

Types of Life Insurance Policies

There are two major categories of life insurance policies; one is called "whole life" or "straight life," and the other is "term insurance."

Term insurance is issued for a term (period of time), usually ranging from one year to ten years. It only protects your family if you die during the term of the policy. Unlike straight life, it does not include savings elements or dividend payments, and you can't cash in a term policy and get money back, because term insurance does not build a cash value. The price or premium for term insurance increases every time you renew the policy. The rate of increase is often specified in advance. In most cases, the premiums (your cost) start out very low relative to whole-life rates, and the increases for renewal are often very reasonable up to age forty-five. When a term policy expires, it is generally worthless; however, during its term it provides insurance at rates which are a fraction of whole-life. Furthermore, as you get older, your earnings usually rise, which makes the increase in term premiums easier to handle. You also have inflation on your side since you pay future premiums with inflated or cheaper dollars. Once you are past the age of forty-five the price of term insurance starts to increase more rapidly than in the early years.

But by age fifty or fifty-five your need for life insurance may have decreased. Term insurance is almost always cheaper than whole-life insurance. A thirty-five-year-old man might take out a $30,000, ten-year-term policy for $150 a year. A $30,000 straight-life or whole-life policy might cost the same man $1,000 a year.

Whole-life insurance. Whole-life policies bought at an early age, before thirty-five or so, may be reasonably priced. But the implied rate of return on your "investment" (the premium you pay) may be very low. Insurance agents often use charts showing that if you pay $1,000 a year, in twenty years you may have $250,000 in cash surrender value. (In other words, that is the sum you would get if you terminated the policy.) This sounds super, rather like instant wealth. But look at the figures more closely. Such a projection implies a 9 percent return on your money. Remember that $1,000 invested for five years at 15 percent, which is not unusual today, will more than double. Investing $1,000 every year at 15 percent will get you more than $500,000 in twenty years. So don't be lulled into a false sense of future prosperity by looking at these tables. Always ask the insurance agent for the implied rate of return that will be earned on the assets, the money you invest. Remember, of course, that you *are* buying life insurance; you are not simply making an investment.

An insurance salesman may claim that whole life amounts to "forced savings" (savings in which the principal is deducted from your paycheck), and in a way this is true. So in considering whether to buy term or whole-life insurance, consider what you could earn by investing the cost difference between the two in a higher-yielding yet safe investment. The value of straight (whole) life insurance should be equal or greater than that of buying term insurance and investing the difference between the premiums.

Term Insurance vs. Straight-Life
Generally speaking, a young family on a limited budget should load up with term insurance and skip straight-life insurance entirely. At age twenty-five, if you can afford to spend $500 a year on a straight-life policy, that may buy $25,000 worth of coverage. But if you put the same $500 in ten-year term insurance, your family could have $150,000 worth of protection for that period. In most cases, the cash value of a straight-life policy grows slowly relative to the premiums, especially in the early years. Also, it

takes many years for that cash value to grow, and in each passing year inflation erodes the value of such "savings."

Insurance companies make more money from straight life than from term. As a result, they offer their agents and salesmen a higher commission for selling straight-life insurance. A typical agent may receive 55 percent of the first year's premium on a straight-life policy, plus 5 percent of the next nine years' premiums. By contrast, on a term policy, the agent may receive 40 percent of the first year's premium and nothing at all thereafter. So when an insurance agent advises you to buy a straight-life (or whole-life) policy or a combination of term and straight, be skeptical. Always be aware that such a sale may suit the agent's needs better than yours. Go ahead and ask him about his commission on the various forms of insurance; you have a right to know.

It may be hard to compare the relative merits of the two kinds of policies because whole-life (or straight-life) policies have a lot of different options and features, and the complexities make it difficult to evaluate the true costs. The best way to deal with this problem is to ask your agent, broker, or salesman if the insurance company subscribes to any independent evaluation service of insurance companies and policies. Evaluation companies compile tables equating the costs of the policies after the benefits and costs of the various features are taken into account. Should your agent not have these tables, write to A.M. Best & Co., Oldwich, New Jersey, 08858. This is the largest independent evaluator. Your local library may also have a copy of *Best's Insurance Reports* or *Best's Review,* a bimonthly periodical.

What Type and How Much?
The following guidelines can help you decide not only what type of insurance you need but also how much.

1. If you are a young single person with no dependents, you do not need life insurance. Some insurance agents tell you to buy a whole life policy when you are young because then you pay

lower premiums; in ten years, they add, you might contract a disease that would make you uninsurable. Of course, you do pay lower premiums when you are young, but your rate of return on those premiums is much lower than you would get from a comparable safe investment, such as bonds, CDs, and treasury bills. And the higher interest you will earn on these other investments can more than compensate you for the increased cost of life insurance when you are older. Besides, very few people in their twenties or thirties are ever turned down by insurance companies for health reasons. When you will need an insurance policy at some future date, you'll probably be able to qualify for one. One word of caution, however: if your family has a history of an illness that tends to strike early, you might hedge your bets and take a small amount of inexpensive renewable term coverage now. You can also buy the right to buy additional insurance in the future no matter what the state of your health by converting your term insurance to straight life.

2. If you are an older single person with no dependents — perhaps, for example, a widow whose children have left home — you also are one of those individuals who may not need life insurance at all. If you have a straight-life policy, keep it only if you wish to leave an estate to your heirs. Otherwise, cash it in and invest the proceeds for a higher income during your own lifetime.

3. If you are a single person with dependents, your insurance needs should be governed by what could happen to them after your death. Divorced parents may expect the children to go to their ex-spouses. If your ex-spouse has enough money to support your children comfortably, you don't need much life insurance. If you want to provide the children with a nest egg, and the property or possessions you own have little value, a small amount of term life insurance may do the trick.

4. If you are married but have no children, and both you and your spouse work, you probably don't need life insurance at all.

If only one spouse provides the family income, that person should have an insurance policy that would cover funeral expenses and give the other spouse a few years' time to begin earning a living on his or her own. In most cases, coverage that provides two to three years of income replacement is adequate. Of course if you choose to insure for continuity of life-style you may elect to purchase more life insurance.

5. If you are married and have minors, then life insurance is essential and probably more so than in any other case. The younger the children, the more insurance you should have, because they need to be covered until they can provide for themselves, which may be a long time. If one parent works, you need enough insurance to protect the other parent too. Think of insurance first as protection and second, when you can afford it, as savings. This means buying mostly term life insurance. Remember that as you grow older, your need for insurance decreases. Now is probably the time when you need the highest level of protection.

6. If you are an older person married to somebody younger with young children, you need as much insurance as any other family breadwinner.

Insurance is a shield of protection for your loved ones, spouse or children. When you have no dependents, you do not need insurance. When your dependents are young or unable to earn income, the need for a protective shield is greatest. As the loved ones approach the stage when they can take care of themselves, the need for this shield decreases.

If you have decided you do need insurance and have selected the type, you face yet another decision: how much insurance to buy. Rely on your own judgment and calculations, because salespeople tend to oversell. And why shouldn't they? The more they sell, the more money they make.

To calculate the amount of insurance you need, answer these questions:

1. What is your annual budget, or how much would your family need for day-to-day living expenses if you died tomorrow? Most insurance experts say that a family needs about 75 percent of its current after-tax income. But if you have grown children or no children at all, your spouse may be able to get along on as little as 50 percent of your current after-tax income.

2. How many years of coverage will your family need? The answer depends on the ages of your children and your spouse's ability to earn a reasonable living after your death. The length of time your family will need the benefit of insurance coverage could vary from one to eighteen years, or more.

3. What income-producing assets do you own? Earnings from such assets could help meet a part of your family's household expenses.

4. What are your survivors' other sources of income? In addition to your spouse's job, if any, and the earnings on your assets, if any, your survivors may be eligible to receive social security, veterans' benefits, and pensions (public or private).

5. Do you have any large outstanding debts? These debts might include a mortgage on your house or other real property, as well as loans outstanding. Even if the surviving spouse could easily carry your present debt load, you may want insurance money to liquidate it.

6. Do you anticipate any major expenditures in the next few years, such as college tuition for children? Although there are ways of meeting tuition costs without using your own money (see early in this section), many of us feel better knowing the cash will be on hand if needed.

7. Do you wish to leave an estate? Some people buy insurance less to pay their survivors' day-to-day living expenses than to leave an estate for their children or their parents, or for a favorite organization or charity.

Now add up everything your family needs to meet its living expenses. Include the mortgage, college costs, time payments, and all other expenses. Subtract the money your family has coming from social security, pensions, salaries, and earnings on such assets as savings and investments. The difference represents the amount of extra income your survivors will need to maintain their present standard of living. Multiply this amount by the number of years your family will need that protection. The result is the amount of insurance you need.

When you consider insurance, keep a few other points in mind. First, state and federal law exempts life insurance death benefits from inheritance taxes. Second, most estates enter probate court, whose processes can take months or years to complete. So your survivors may have to wait until the proceeds of your estate are distributed. Life insurance, on the other hand, becomes available to the beneficiary immediately after the policyholder's death. Third, at any time, and at no additional cost, you can change the beneficiaries of your life insurance policy or revise the terms under which the proceeds are to be paid. A lawyer, on the other hand, charges you each time you change your will.

One final point: when you need it, insurance should be a first priority. Take care of your insurance needs before investing in any assets, no matter how safe.

The Strategy

The aim of this cost-saving strategy is to help you buy the optimum amount of insurance at the best price. Based on what you now know:

1. Calculate the amount of insurance you currently need.

2. Shop for rates on both whole life and term. Get cost estimates from a number of insurance agents, preferably including at least two who compare favorably in Best's publications.

3. The amount of insurance you need, the cost differences of the various policies, and the cost of premiums you can afford to pay determine the single type of insurance or proportional mix of whole life and term that is best for you.

4. Now that you know the amount, the type, and the proportion, capitalize on your knowledge by getting the best policy.

Owning the right type of insurance at the best price brings very large cost savings as well as peace of mind.

Tax Savings

We've already noted (in Section I) that the best way to evaluate the return on any investment is to look at what will be left over after inflation and after taxes. Controlling inflation is beyond the ability of any individual; controlling your level of taxes is not, for you can take advantage of quite a wide range of tax breaks.

Keeping your tax bill down starts with keeping careful records — records, among other things, of every exclusion, deduction, and tax break allowed under the law. The following items are fully deductible expenses which are associated with investing:

- Margin account interest
- State transfer taxes
- Safe deposit box costs, if you use the box to store any assets related to investing
- The cost of investment books, newspapers, magazines, and other periodicals, as well as tax publications
- Investment counseling and advisory service fees
- Fees for advisers and tax accountants
- All postage and telephone calls associated with investing
- All brokerage commissions

Brokerage commissions, on both purchases and sales, are part of your investment costs. As such, correctly accounting for commissions for tax purposes can reduce your tax bite. If you sell your securities at a gain, the commission costs reduce the amount of tax you must pay; they will also add to your loss and therefore your tax credit, if you sell securities that have declined in value.

Short- and Long-Term Gains

Each time you buy a security, accurately record the date of purchase and the amount paid, so you will be able to distinguish between short- and long-term gains and losses. To qualify for a long-term capital gain or loss, you must have held an investment for a year and a day; a short-term capital gain or loss is used for an investment held for less than a year and a day. In general, try to realize capital gains on a long-term rather than short-term basis. The reason is that the entire short-term capital gain is taxed as ordinary income, whereas 60 percent of a net long-term capital gain is excluded from taxation. The remaining 40 percent of the net long-term gain is taxable at your ordinary income tax rate, up to a maximum of 50 percent. Thus, if you have a long-term capital gain of $1,000, $600 is exempt from taxation. The remaining $400 is taxed at your regular rate, but you will never pay more than $200 (50 percent of 40 percent of $1,000). That means that the effective long-term capital gains tax can be no higher than 20 percent (50 percent of 40 percent).

Here is an example of how to figure short- and long-term capital gains and losses. First, determine your net *long-term* capital gains or losses and then your net *short-term* capital gains or losses. Suppose you have a long-term gain of $5,000 and a long-term loss of $2,000. Your *net* long-term gain is $2,000 subtracted from $5,000, or $3,000. Now assume that you have $2,000 in short-term gains and $3,000 in short-term losses. This means that your net short-term loss ($3,000 minus $2,000) is $1,000. To determine your *net* capital gain, subtract the $1,000 net short-term loss from the $3,000 net long-term gain, and you have a net long-term gain of

$2,000. (A net short-term gain equals the sum you have left after you subtract from your total gains all short-term losses and long-term losses, and it is taxed as ordinary income.)

Because short- and long-term gains and losses are treated differently, you must properly identify the securities you sell if you want to get the highest possible tax break. Well-kept records enable you to keep track of your assets and are especially useful if you own a number of different stocks or a number of lots of the same stock. (A lot is a specific purchase of a stock. If you buy 100 shares of ABC Company at $20 on one day, and another 100 shares at $18 the next day, you own two different lots of the ABC stock.) When you sell, if you cannot or do not identify the specific lot you are selling, the IRS assumes that you sold the first lot (first in–first out). Choosing which lot to declare can have a tremendous impact on your tax bill. A short-term gain can become a long-term gain; a gain can become a loss for tax purposes. Keeping track of the different lots is particularly important in the case of strategies which involve buying several lots of the same stock, such as dollar averaging.

The significance of declaring the lot of your choice can be illustrated through the following example: You own 300 shares of GGG Company. One hundred shares were purchased at $10 a share, the next 100 shares at $20, the last 100 shares at $30 a share.

The price of the stock is currently $20 a share. You have some minor misgivings about the company and decide to lighten up by selling 100 shares. If you "declare" the first lot, you will show a capital gain of $1,000, which will be taxed. If you "sell" the second lot, you will have no gains or losses. If you "sell" the third lot, you will show a $1,000 capital loss.

If you had not declared the lot, the IRS would assume you sold the first lot and you would have to pay tax on the $1,000 gain. Depending on your other investment experiences that year and your top-dollar tax bracket, the disparity between a $1,000 gain and a $1,000 loss can make a big difference in the size of your tax bite.

Confirmations from your broker will enable you to identify the various lots; however, using the purchases and sales statement (in Section III) may save you hours of searching at tax time.

To further minimize your taxes, base decisions as to which lot to sell on your taxable income, as well as on the capital gains or losses you "booked" (realized) during the tax year. Suppose you own 100 shares of ABC Corporation, purchased at $20 each, two years ago. Nine months ago, however, you bought an additional 100 shares at $30 a share. Assume that then you sold 100 shares of ABC stock at $25 a share. As a result, you can show either a $5 long-term capital gain or a $5 short-term capital loss on each share, depending on which lot you declare. The decision whether to take the capital gain or the capital loss will depend on whether you had a net gain or a net loss for the year.

Another point to keep in mind is that capital losses on securities can be used to offset capital gains on other investments, such as jewelry, real estate, and art. Many inexperienced investors overlook this point and as a result miss opportunities to save on taxes.

Dividend and Interest Exclusions and All-Savers

Current federal income tax law allows you to exclude the first $200 in dividends or interest from your taxable income — $400 for a joint return if the couple owns the stocks or if each received at least $200 in qualifying dividends.

In addition, a new tax shelter vehicle has been created: the all-savers certificate. The all-savers permits you to exclude from taxation up to $1,000 in interest from certificates issued by qualifying financial institutions between October 1, 1981, and December 31, 1982. For couples filing jointly, the exclusion doubles to $2,000. The certificates are issued for a twelve-month period, but the interest exclusion is available to taxpayers for more than two years because interest earned on certificates issued before December 31, 1982, will remain tax-free up to December 31, 1983. The interest on all-savers certificates is 70 percent of the fifty-two-week treasury bill rate in the month the certificates are issued. If an investor buys an all-savers when the interest rate on fifty-two-week treasury bills is 15 percent, the all-savers' rate will be 10.5 percent. Once it is purchased, though, the rate remains fixed during the entire one-year period. To discourage early withdrawals, the interest will be fully taxed in the event these certificates are redeemed before the year is up. Because of this some banks are issuing certificates in $500 units. This way, if you need cash quickly, you can cash in one or two of these policies and pay taxes only on the interest earned on the amount withdrawn. For example, if you invest $8,238, you will receive 16 units of $500 each and one unit of $238, the last unit almost always being an odd amount. You may only receive one physical document, but the computer knows that you have seventeen separate units.

The $1,000 once-in-a-lifetime exemption need not be taken all in one year. If you think interest rates are going to rise further, or if you are currently unable to invest the maximum, postpone a part of your purchase. You have until December 31, 1982.

While banks tout all-savers as a bit of a miracle, these certificates are not for everybody. You can make more money from an all-savers certificate than from buying a t-bill outright only if your marginal tax rate is more than 30 percent. Furthermore, the amount you invest must be calculated carefully in order to insure that the earnings do not exceed the maximum interest exclusion. Any interest over $1,000 per person (or $2,000 per couple filing a joint return) is subject to taxation. You can compute the maximum amount it pays for you to invest by dividing the maximum tax-free interest ($1,000 or $2,000) by the rate of interest offered on the day you buy an all-savers. For example, a couple who file a joint income tax return and buy an all-savers yielding 10.5 percent must limit their total investment to $19,048 ($2,000 ÷ 0.105) to gain the greatest possible benefit. The following table shows maximum investments at different interest levels:

	10.5%	12.5%	14.5%
One person	$ 9,524	$ 8,000	$ 6,897
Couple filing jointly	19,048	16,000	13,793

Many banks require a minimum purchase of $500 but thereafter will issue certificates in any amount.

Whether you should invest in an all-savers certificate or in a taxable instrument depends on your marginal tax bracket. The following table compares the before-tax and after-tax yields of a one-year taxable CD paying 16 percent interest with the tax-exempt yield of an all-savers paying 12 percent interest.

1982 Marginal Tax Bracket (Federal Tax Only)	Investment*	Pretax Yield	Interest	Tax	After-Tax Yield
20 percent	All-savers	12	$1,000	0	12.0
	1-year CD	16	$1,333	267	12.8
30 percent	All-savers	12	$1,000	0	12.0
	1-year CD	16	$1,333	933	11.2
40 percent	All-savers	12	$1,000	0	12.0
	1-year CD	16	$1,333	533	9.6
50 percent	All-savers	12	$1,000	0	12.0
	1-year CD	18	$1,333	666	8.0

*Amount invested is $8,333.

In this example it would be more profitable to buy the 16 percent taxable CD only in the first case. In fact it would pay for you to buy this CD if your marginal tax rate was less than 25 percent.

Bear in mind that a money market fund or a three-month t-bill would keep your money more liquid (available to you) than either a CD or an all-savers, but CDs, t-bills, and money market funds do not provide the same tax break. The interest of a money market fund is fully taxed as ordinary income, while the interest on a treasury bill is subject only to federal tax.

Reading between the lines. In connection with our discussion of all-savers, I am reminded of the part that advertising sometimes plays in dispensing biased information.

You probably saw full-page advertisements last year (1981) for what was then a new kind of investment instrument — the all-savers certificate. I first saw one of these ads on a morning when I was trying to do too much work in too little time. But habit made me flip through the financial section of the morning paper. Then I saw it — an ad for an all-savers. "Earn 40 percent a year!" I looked again. Not even Paul Voelker (chairman of the Federal Reserve) at his most dismal ever predicted interest rates of 40 percent. Why, the prime had closed the day before at 19¾ percent! I started to read the entire advertisement word for word and line by line. Quite a learning experience.

Yes, an investor would in a sense earn 40 percent annually, but there was a small but important catch: the 40 percent rate was not for the all-savers itself, but for an investment instrument that would be converted into an all-savers in about a month's time. The bank guaranteed the rate of 0.11 percent a day (which is 40 percent a year) only for the month of September 1981. But beginning October 1, 1981, the bank would put the money into an all-savers certificate — and not at 40 percent, but at 70 percent of whatever rate of return U.S. treasury bills were offering on a particular day. On October 1, treasury bills were paying 18 percent. The bank would place the investor's money in all all-savers paying 12.6 percent (70 percent of 18 percent), not 40 percent. Still, the claim of 40 percent annual interest was perfectly legal, because the Truth-in-Lending law requires that interest rates be quoted in terms of annual percentages; and at the time the ads for these instruments appeared, they were indeed offering annual rates of 40 percent per year, even though the offer was good for only one month.

As I read further into the advertisement, the print got finer. It seemed that the first $1,000 (for an individual) or $2,000 (for a couple filing a joint return) of earnings from the new instruments would be excluded from income tax. Better than nothing, of course; but the ad didn't say that interest over that level would be taxed at the investor's top-dollar rate. For this reason it would not have paid at the time for anyone to invest more than $7,936 in an all-savers.

The ad was perfectly legal, despite its misrepresentations. Still, not everything was quite all right. The IRS eventually ruled that the initial high rate could not be tied to the requirement that on October 1 the funds be invested in an all-savers; it granted the investor the right to withdraw the funds altogether.

Banks offered these incentives because they want and need your money — especially the savings banks that have been lending thirty-year mortgage money at low rates until quite recently. Mortgage money is long-term money. A large portion of these banks' assets is earning them returns at far lower rates than they have to pay for new money, which is leaving these banks in a margin squeeze. The introduction of the all-saver certificate was an opportunity to increase their deposits.

What the law doesn't say. The omissions of the Truth-in-Lending law can create complications for the holders of credit cards, too, and I must admit that I myself was once a victim. Since I want to avoid interest charges and penalties on my credit card, I pay the bill each month in full. But I had never bothered to read the fine print on my credit card agreement, and that was my mistake.

One month, my bill was $898. I paid it promptly, but in doing so I transposed the "9" and the "8" and so wrote a check for $889. When the next month's bill arrived, I noticed a charge of $13.47 under interest. By this time I had discovered the transposition, so I was not surprised to be paying interest. But $13.47? As I pointed out to the bank that issued the card, that was 150 percent a month, or 1,796 percent a year, on a current outstanding balance of $9 ($898 less $889). The bank promptly pointed out to me that $13.47 represented 1½ percent a month (18 percent a year) of the *entire* previous balance — $898 — rather than the current outstanding balance.

Had I read the fine print I'd have known this. The bank can get away with murder because the Truth-in-Lending law specifies that customers must be informed of the *annual* percentage rate of interest they are paying but does not concern itself with the method of determining the *balance* on which that interest is charged.

I've already discussed (in Section II) lending companies that are not so well regulated and perhaps even more unethical. Anyone who deals with these organizations must understand precisely what interest is charged on what balance, for what period of time. But not only must you read what is stated in fine print; you must also think about what is not printed at all. "What am I really getting?" "What does it really cost?" "What am I giving up?" "What are my alternatives?" "What are they not telling me?" So remember, if you do not understand, ask. If you still do not understand, ask again. And if after a time you still do not understand, don't do it. There is probably a reason why your questions cannot be answered simply, a reason that may cause you regret later on.

I know that it is not easy for most people to ask questions; that's why so many of us become victims of pressure and intimidation. Try to develop a bit of what is known as chutzpa — nerve, gall, the guts to stand up and demand your rights. All of us can use a little more chutzpa where money is concerned.

Retirement Accounts

Individual retirement account (IRA). An IRA is a personal pension fund, a fund into which you can put pretax dollars that earn tax-deferred interest. This personal pension fund is taxed only when you withdraw money. If you wait until retirement to withdraw your money, your tax rate may be lower, and in the meantime your money is working all for you.

Tom Howard is a chief clerk for a large corporation close to his home. He earns an excellent salary, and the firm gives him an attractive package of fringe benefits, including a pension plan. That's why Tom and his wife, Sally, could not take advantage of the tax savings offered by IRAs when they were first introduced. As of January 1, 1982, however, the restriction was eliminated. IRAs are no longer limited to people who are not covered by a private or government pension program; now *all* employed persons are eligible. Furthermore, you can invest up to $2,000 a year in such an account — no matter what proportion that might be of your total income.

Tom decided to open an IRA and to make the maximum annual contribution allowed by law, $2,000. Furthermore, though Sally is not gainfully employed, she and her husband file a joint income tax return, which means that Tom can add an additional $250 to his IRA account for her.

Assuming that the Howards make the highest annual contribution now allowed, $2,250, they automatically reduce their gross taxable income by that amount and thereby save the taxes they would otherwise have to pay on that amount. If they withdraw any amount from an IRA before age 59½, they pay a 10 percent penalty in addition to the tax due on the amount withdrawn. This penalty is not as serious as it looks, though, because at today's interest rates they made up that 10 percent penalty in the first year because of the tax-deferred yield on the pretax dollars in the IRA.

Remember, by opening an IRA you are putting away pretax dollars earning tax-deferred interest.

Keogh Plan (H.R.-10). According to Internal Revenue regulations, Barbara Huile qualifies as "self-employed." A talented artist, she has converted her garage into a studio and, with a bit of discreet advertising and many word-of-mouth recommendations, has established herself as a portrait painter. Now the well-heeled pay well for a "Portrait by Huile."

Back in 1975, when Keoghs were introduced, Barbara rushed to open one, and each year since, she has made the maximum allowable contribution. A Keogh Plan is a personal retirement fund (pension fund) for people who are self-employed. How will the new Keogh tax laws affect her?

The new tax act doubled the maximum deductible amount that can be put into a Keogh Plan each year, from $7,500 to $15,000, so long as no more than 15 percent of one's earned income goes into the account. Further, the new law allows a self-employed person with a Keogh Plan to put an additional $2,000 into an IRA. This raises to $17,000 the maximum amount that can be put into a tax-deferred retirement account in any one year.

The Benefits of IRAs and Keoghs

IRAs and Keoghs offer substantial benefits for two reasons. First, in neither fund is the money deposited taxed, so more money is working for the investor at all times. Second, no tax is due on the income or capital gains earned from either type of account until the actual date of withdrawal.

The impact, even in the most limited cases, is that the return on the investment increases by anywhere from 110 to 300 percent, depending on one's tax bracket. For example, a person in the 30 percent marginal tax bracket invests $2,000 in an IRA. The investment instrument chosen is a certificate of deposit paying 18 percent. The investor earns $360 the first year, which for the present is exempt from taxes. The following year, the investor has $2,360 earning interest.

Had this investor put the same money into a taxable investment, the 30 percent tax on the initial $2,000 would have come to $600, leaving only $1,400 available for further investment. The interest on $1400 earned on an 18 percent CD would come to only $252 and would be taxed as ordinary income. In the end, only $176.40 would be "free and clear," a mere 8.8 percent of the original $2,000! Let's compare: 18 percent with an IRA, 8.8 percent without one; $2,360 earning interest next year with an IRA, $1,576 without one.

Since the interest earned on IRAs and Keoghs is not taxed, one should lean strongly toward investing in high-yielding instruments. But these should also be no-risk or low-risk investments, since the purpose of these accounts is to supplement income after retirement — which is why, by the way, investors are penalized 10 percent for withdrawing from their accounts before age 59½. Withdraw $1,000 and the government takes $100. Furthermore, the sum withdrawn is subject to full income tax at the time of withdrawal. But as previously mentioned, this 10 percent penalty can be made up in the first year of investing.

The following table dramatizes the effect of compounding interest (collecting interest on interest) on a $1,000 investment. As you can see, doubling the interest far more than doubles the return. If your top-dollar tax rate is 50 percent, you double the interest by putting money in an IRA or a Keogh. In addition, the compounding is further enhanced by investing pretax money.

GROWTH OF $1,000

Rate of Interest	Ten Years	Twenty Years
5.0%	$1,630	$ 2,650
7.5%	$2,060	$ 4,248
10.0%	$2,600	$ 6,730
12.5%	$3,250	$10,545
15.0%	$4,045	$16,370
18.5%	$5,015	$25,162
20.0%	$6,200	$38,340

This table can also be used when examining life insurance return tables to better understand their increased value over a long term. However you may use it, never discount the importance of earning interest on interest; even more so if it is exempt from taxation.

There is another interesting way to reduce your tax bite: shifting assets to another person, one who is in a much lower tax bracket. This strategy can provide a means of helping elderly parents, or it can help you reduce the cost of putting your children through college. Two ways of transferring income to reduce taxes are a Clifford Trust and an interest-free demand loan.

Clifford Trusts

A Clifford Trust is a trust which is set up for a minimum of ten years. During that time it cannot be revoked. The income from the trust is taxable to the beneficiary of the trust. Since the beneficiary is presumably in a lower tax bracket than you are, the tax on the income is lower also. For example, if you had $20,000 invested in government bonds yielding 15 percent, you would earn $3,000 a year in interest. Assuming you are in the 50 percent marginal tax bracket, you would pay $1,500 in taxes, which would leave you with $1,500. Had you put these bonds in a Clifford Trust for a child with an income of under $3,400 a year, there would be no taxes due at all. The full $3,000 would remain intact, earning interest, instead of just $1,500.

At the end of the term, the trust dissolves and you get back your assets.

Interest-Free Demand Loan

The second strategy is an interest-free demand loan. Currently (1982), this strategy is accepted by the IRS. However, the IRS has been trying to litigate the issue. It has had no success thus far, but before you act, consult a lawyer or accountant as to whether the status has changed. Interest-free demand loans are no-interest loans, payable on demand. The borrower can place the money in a high-yielding investment (such as that 15 percent bond) and be taxed at lower rates than the lender. If the borrower earns more than $3,400 there will be some tax due. Since this is a demandable loan, you can demand repayment of all or part of the loan if you need the money in the interim. The advantage of this strategy over the Clifford Trust is its flexibility. Not only can you issue this loan for whatever term you want, but you can always get your money back when you need it. It may be advisable to accept repayment of small portions of the loan. In most states, if after six years there has been no repayment activity, a loan may be considered a "bad debt," and therefore invalidated.

But what if you don't have the money to take advantage of any of these strategies? You can always borrow against your assets. Remember, interest costs are tax-deductible to you. To find out whether it will pay for you to borrow, compare your after-tax cost of borrowing (using your top-dollar tax rate) to the after-tax return to the beneficiary.

No-Risk Strategies

And now, readers, we come to my favorite part of the book; my favorite because no-risk strategies are simple, easy-to-execute, complete strategies. You can easily line up all the possibilities, and you can measure the results very precisely. These strategies are also fun, because they turn you into an investigator.

As we described them in the previous section, safe investments include treasury bills, treasury notes, government bonds, high-grade (AAA and AA) corporate bonds, agency bonds, certificates of deposit, money market funds, and high-grade commercial paper. Below is a table that makes it easier for you to keep track of your findings. The most accessible sources of information for filling out the table are local newspapers, financial newspapers, the library, and your stockbroker. Among the periodicals and financial newspapers that contain this information are the *Wall Street Journal,* published every business day; *Barron's,* published on Saturday; and the *New York Times.*

If you have brokers who are willing to give you these rates of return over the phone, by all means call them; it will save you the time of looking up this information yourself. (Calling a broker for information in no way obligates you to transact business with him or the firm he represents.) Despite the convenience of relying on a broker, I do suggest that you do some of your own research just so you'll learn how to do it yourself. Most newspapers have tables in the financial section called "Consumer Rates," "Rates Available to Consumers," or "Key Rates" that list a number of important average interest rates. This table will generally include the passbook savings rate at savings institutions, the average six-month CD rate, three-month and six-month t-bills, seven-year treasury notes, thirty-year treasury bonds, an index of corporate bonds, and an index of municipals or tax-exempt bonds. Some papers also include the seven-day-average money market fund rate, rates on various unsecured loans, and the prime rate.

The table on page 161 will help you to stay abreast of the returns or interest that can be earned on safe, fixed-income sources. If you cannot locate the rates called for in the following chart, try to find a proxy; for example, a proxy for a long-term bond is a long-term bond index. A proxy for a ten-year bond is an index with an average maturity of eight to twelve years.

In case you haven't guessed yet, the no-risk strategy consists of borrowing money at low interest rates and investing it at higher interest rates. If you borrowed $10,000 at 12 percent per year and invested it at 16 percent per year, you would have a 4 percent incremental return — a pretax "gift" of 4 percent, or $400 for every year that your strategy is "locked in."

Now that you know what interest rates are available, you must choose the length of time that you wish to employ the risk-free strategy. If you buy a three-month treasury bill, you will be assured that the incremental return will last for three months. If, on the other hand, you are willing to buy a five-year bond, you have ensured that the strategy will work for five years. Before choosing, consider the following questions:

1. Where do you expect interest rates to go in the future? If you expect them to rise over the short term, you want to ensure the strategy for a shorter period of time. After all, the money you have borrowed will still be yours later on, and then you may be able to lock in even higher returns. Conversely, if you expect interest rates to drop in the next year or two, then buy a longer-term instrument. Note, however, that investment professionals as well as economists have a very hard time predicting the direction or the magnitude of interest rate changes.

2. What is the current interest-rate structure — in other words, the difference in interest between short-term and long-term securities?

As we look over the last fifty or sixty years, interest rates for shorter instruments — that is, CDs and t-bills — generally have

INTEREST TABLES

	Current Yield or Interest	Yield to Maturity
Short-Term		
Money market mutual funds	_____	_____
T-bills	_____	_____
CDs	_____	_____
Savings accounts	_____	_____
_____	_____	_____
_____	_____	_____
Intermediate		
5-year CD	_____	_____
5-year treasury note (gov't)	_____	_____
5-year AA corporate	_____	_____
10-year treasury note (gov't)	_____	_____
10-year AA corporate	_____	_____
_____	_____	_____
_____	_____	_____
Long-Term		
20-year treasury bond (gov't)	_____	_____
20-year AA corporate	_____	_____
30-year treasury bond (gov't)	_____	_____
30-year AA corporate	_____	_____
_____	_____	_____
_____	_____	_____

been lower than those on longer-term instruments. The underlying assumption has been that the longer the term, the more risk of future uncertainty one has to bear. Consequently, the investor expects to earn higher interest rates in order to be compensated for that increased risk. But during the past few years we have had an inverted yield curve. Short-term instruments have earned a higher rate of interest than longer-term instruments. This indicates that investors have had more confidence in the long-term economy than in short-term events.

One further point to keep in mind is that there is no reason to put all of your money into the instrument paying the highest return. By the same token, you do not have to invest all your borrowed money to mature at the same time. If the highest paying instrument is a one-year CD, you may choose to put part of your borrowed money into that instrument and the rest into a five-year bond. By doing this you are locking in a lower rate of return on a portion of the money, but you lock it in for a longer period of time. In some cases you may want to match the maturity of the loan with the maturity of the bond so that they both come due at the same time — especially if your loan is due in full at the end of the term.

Implicit in all these risk-free strategies are three assumptions:

1. You will hold the security to maturity or will only sell it at a price equal to or higher than the price you paid for it.

2. The duration of your loan will be equal to or greater than the maturity of your investment.

3. Either your loan is not due in full until the end of the period; or, if it is an installment loan, you have the money to pay the monthly payments.

These assumptions help you to avoid having to liquidate the investment before it matures. Pressure to sell before maturity may expose you to the risks of price fluctuations. The optimal or best time periods for you will depend on the type of repayment arrangements you have with your lender, as well as the tradeoffs among the levels of interest rates for different maturities.

Now that you have chosen the time periods, get out the list of money sources and the list of rates on safe fixed-income investments. The strategy is very simple. Borrow as much money as you can at the lowest rates and invest the proceeds in those securities with the highest interest rates so long as the rates at which you invest are higher than the rates at which you borrow, and your investment will mature in time to permit you to pay back your loan. Simple, isn't it? Let's consider a few examples.

EXAMPLE 1:

You borrow $10,000 from a low-cost source for five years at 12 percent interest. The $10,000 principal is due in full at the end of the five years. Your best bet is to buy a five-year government note or a corporate bond. You may also want to pay the interest each year. Doing so will help reduce the tax bite on your interest income.

EXAMPLE 2:

You borrow $5,000 from your profit-sharing plan at 10 percent for three years. This loan must be paid in monthly installments. If you do not have the money to pay the monthly installments, you may either (1) put the money into a money market fund (so long as its interest rate exceeds 10 percent); or (2) put $1,000 into a money market fund in order to pay the first year's installments, and with the remainder buy four $1,000 CDs or bonds with maturities of one year, eighteen months, two years and three years respectively. You will lock in your profits, and as these certificates mature, you will have the money to continue to pay the installments.

EXAMPLE 3:

You borrow $10,000 against the cash value of your life insurance policy at 8 percent. In most cases such loans have no due date. If such is the case, you may invest the proceeds in any fixed-income instrument with any maturity; or, for that matter, in any number of securities, each with a different maturity. And pay the interest on the loan every year, to get the tax deduction and avoid paying interest on interest.

WARNING:

Do not invest borrowed money in tax-free investments such as all-savers or municipal bonds. The IRS disallows tax deductions for interest paid on loans invested in tax-exempt vehicles. This rule also applies to tax-deferred vehicles such as IRAs and Keoghs.

Interest rates may rise or fall, but the no-risk strategies work until the lowest cost of borrowing additional funds equals the highest rate available for investments.

Low- to Medium-Risk Strategies

Risk can be measured, or at least approximated. But "low" or "medium" risk is really a value judgment. What is low risk to one person may be high risk to another.

Yet the low- to medium-risk strategies described in this section do control and reduce the risk of losing money invested in stocks and in intermediate and long-term bonds.

Common Stock and Common Sense

Before you buy a stock — any stock or a group of stocks — you should have a clear and logical reason for believing the stock's price will go up. You may choose a company that produces high-quality products or goods that are in high demand, or a company which is well positioned to take advantage of the current and future economic trends. For example, "My friends and I love the new products of the Beauty-Beele Soap and Cosmetics Company. We also like the way they package and sell their products. And we think others will like it too." Or, "The Computer Game Company has a wonderful new computer toy that's been sold out in most of the stores where I've looked for it." Or, "I think interest rates are going to go down substantially, and since utility companies' earnings are closely related to interest costs, I think Gaslight Utility Company may be in a good position over the next few years."

You may want to seek out and investigate new potential investments on your own, or you may want to rely on your broker. If you do your own homework, you will not need to consult your broker for investment "ideas" and therefore you may want to use a discount broker. If, on the other hand, you will require research advice and analysis, use a full-service broker. Remember, though, that published information such as quality ratings and historical dividend and earnings growth records may be available from a discount broker as well as a full-service firm.

If at any time the clear, logical reasons that led you to buy the stock change, consider selling the stock. It is not enough to believe that XYZ Company is a good company. You should have a specific reason for thinking that current earnings are likely to improve, by how much, and when.

Choosing a Bond
The three major decisions for you to make before buying a long-term bond are:

1. How important to you is current yield?

2. What maturity is best for you?

3. What quality bond?

Since bond prices adjust to overall yield-to-maturity levels, the lower the price of the bond (relative to par and maturity), the lower the current yield, because the capital gain you will receive at maturity is factored into yield-to-maturity but not into current yield.

You will be choosing either a discount bond (one selling at

below $1,000), a par bond (selling at par or $1,000), or a premium bond (selling at over $1,000).

Discount vs. premium bonds. The difference between discount bonds and premium bonds is the price relative to the face value or par value. A discount bond sells below $1,000, whereas a premium bond sells above $1,000. Assuming that these bonds have similar maturities, qualities and issuers, their yield to maturity will be roughly the same. However, the *current yield* on a discount bond will be far lower than the current yield on the premium bond. This occurs because with the discount bond you will have a capital gain at maturity, and with the premium bond you will have a capital loss at maturity. Yield to maturity reflects capital changes as well as interest income, while current yield is simply coupon divided by current price.

Example:

Bond A and Bond B are both AAA corporate, maturing in five years.

Bond A has a coupon of 16 percent and is selling at $110.

Bond B has a coupon of 4 percent and is selling at $64.

The pretax yield to maturity on both bonds is about the same, 15.4 percent. On the other hand, the current yield on Bond A is 14.5 percent ($160 coupon ÷ $1,100 price), while the current yield on Bond B is 6.25 percent ($40 ÷ $640).

As we discussed in Section III, these price and current yield differentials depend on the coupon of a bond and the prevailing yield-to-maturity levels. A thirty-year bond issued twenty years ago will have the same yield to maturity as a ten-year bond issued today, all other things being equal.

Which should you buy, a premium bond or a discount bond? Your choice depends on your tax bracket and your need for current income. Remember that the IRS regards interest as normal income and the price differential between current price and value at maturity as a capital gain or loss. If your tax situation calls for capital gains treatment, and you do not need the current income for living, then you have good reason to buy a discount bond.

At today's historically high interest rates, there are very few premium bonds. However, a premium bond would be a good investment for a person who needs current income, since premium bonds are high-coupon bonds.

Maturity. The appropriate bond maturities for you depend on your investment time horizon, when you may need the money, and in what direction you expect interest rates to go.

Quality. The lower the quality, the riskier the bond. Bonds rated AAA, AA, or even A afford ample assurance of asset coverage for the average investor. Historically, the bonds at the lower end of the quality spectrum have offered higher returns to those willing to take the extra risk. But these bonds also do tend to be more volatile. Let's examine the characteristics of different kinds of bonds by looking at a few bond quotations selected from a recent publication.

On page 168 are ten- and twenty-year bonds from different quality categories. Because long-term rates were at near-historic highs, there were few premium bonds. All the bond issues in this example were selling at a discount from par.

You will note that:
- As the quality of the issue decreases, yield to maturity increases. This is how low-quality bond holders are rewarded for the increased risk.
- The longer bond within each quality group has a higher yield to maturity, in line with traditional expectations.
- Current yield varies from 9.6 percent to 15.3 percent.

Current yield vs. capital gain or price appreciation; personal comfort with quality ratings; and length of maturity of issue are the three prime criteria in selecting a bond.

If you are risk-averse and do not need high current income, you might choose the ten-year NNN bond.

If lower quality does not disturb you and you want a high current income, you may choose the twenty-year RRR or TTT bond.

(1) Quality	(2) Name, Coupon and Maturity	(3) Current Price	(4) Current Yield	(5) Yield To Maturity
A A A	LLL 7.15 — 10 yr.	65½	10.9	13.8
A A A	MMN 8.75 — 20 yr.	63½	13.8	14.3
A A	NNN 4.875 — 10 yr.	51	9.6	14.3
A A	PPP 8.75 — 20 yr.	63	13.9	14.5
A	QQQ 4.5 — 10 yr.	46	9.8	14.9
A	RRR 7.375 — 20 yr.	51	14.4	15.0
B a a	SSS 4.875 — 10 yr.	47½	10.3	15.4
B a a	TTT 7.625 — 20 yr.	50	15.3	16.1

Column (1): Quality — Moody's quality ratings.
    (2): Name, Coupon and Maturity — Fictitious name of issuing company; coupon should be multiplied by 10 to arrive at dollar amount; maturity indicates the year of repayment of $1,000 bond value.
    (3): Current Price — Multiply by 10 to arrive at cost.
    (4): Current Yield — Coupon ÷ current price.
    (5): Yield to Maturity — Comprises all future dividend payments and includes *ultimate* price appreciation.

Types of Orders

Buying or selling a stock or a bond requires placing an order with the broker. There are many different types of orders. You may even place simultaneous orders to buy or sell the same investment at different prices. In fact, some of our strategies require placing a number of orders at one time.

Here is a description of the types of orders you will be using:

1. *A market order.* An order to buy or sell a stock at the going

market price is called a market order. The price at which you will buy or sell the stock is the price of the stock on the floor of the exchange at the *moment* your broker executes that order. Usually, the price won't have changed by more than ¼ to ½ point (25 to 50 cents) per share of stock from the time you place your order until the trade is executed. To make sure your orders have been reasonably well carried out, check the evening paper for the highs and lows of the day. By doing this, you will learn whether or not your broker executed the order within those limits. If not, contact him immediately for an explanation. You may even be entitled to a refund.

2. *A limit order* (also called *a stop order*). This is an order to buy or sell a stock or bond at a particular price. If you own a stock which is currently selling at $25, you may want to sell it when it goes down by 10 percent. Therefore, you place a sell-limit order for that stock at $22.50. If the stock's price goes down to that limit price, the stock is instantaneously sold. You can also place a limit order to buy a stock at a particular price. If the current price is $25 and you feel the stock may go lower, in order to buy the stock at a cheaper price you may want to put a buy-limit order for the purchase of additional shares of the stock at $22.50. If the price subsequently goes down to $22.50, you will have bought the stock at a 10 percent savings from the day that you put in your order. Keep in mind, however, that should the stock not reach that precise level, your order will not be executed and the stock may "run away" from you — go up without dipping to $22.50. Oh, well, there are lots of other fish in the sea.

If you own that same $25 stock and you want to ensure that you realize a profit, you can put in a limit order to sell the shares when they reach $35, locking in a 40 percent price appreciation; or at $50 a share, a 100 percent profit. Of course, again, if the stock never reaches the exact "stop" ($35 or $50 a share), the order is never executed.

3. *Same-day orders.* Orders which must be executed within the day they are placed are called same-day orders. Market orders are same-day orders, as are some limit orders.

4. *The good-till-canceled order.* This is an order that stays on the books either until it is fulfilled or until it is canceled by the client. Most limit or stop orders are good-till-canceled orders.

There is one more point, a very subtle one: If you think the stock may go lower in price, but at the same time you don't want it to "get away" from you if it does not, you will want to place a limit-buy order for that stock at 5 or 10 percent above the current market price to cover the possibility that you may be wrong. At the same time, place a limit order at 10 percent below the current market price. You may end up paying more for the stock, but you will own it before its price really runs up very much.

Mutual Funds

Mutual funds are pools of assets which are professionally invested. These funds own large numbers of securities and are therefore much more diversified than any single investment. Mutual funds come in all sizes and types, ranging from money market funds to bond funds to stock funds to real estate funds. The common stock funds range from conservative (high income) to aggressive growth.

Load vs. no-load mutual funds. A load is a sales charge. Some funds add a load fee of up to 12 percent to the price of the shares. This load is the salesman's commission, which is subtracted from your total investment, leaving that much less money at work for you. The salesman who calls you on the phone or offers to visit with you is probably selling a load mutual fund.

No-load funds have no sales charge, leaving the entire amount available for investment. No-load funds are bought directly from the fund management. Historically, there has been no difference in the aggregate performance between load and no-load funds.

Therefore, if you know how to select an appropriate no-load mutual fund by yourself, you can save the sales charge or load, and end up that much ahead.

Open-end vs. closed-end funds. Open-end funds increase the number of shares with each new cash inflow, and decrease the number with each new outflow. Therefore the fund grows as people put in money and shrinks when the money is withdrawn.

Closed-end (publicly traded) funds, like all mutual funds, are diversified, are professionally managed, and have various investment objectives. However, the difference between open-end and closed-end funds is that there is a fixed number of shares in a closed-end fund; the price of the shares is determined by demand and therefore fluctuates up and down past its net asset value, just as ordinary common stocks do. Historically, closed-end funds have sold at either discounts or premiums from their net asset values.

Open-end funds offer investors a greater flexibility and range in buying options. There are many more investment programs from which to choose, such as automatic reinvestment or withdrawal plans and automatic dividend reinvestment.

Mutual fund — strategy or investment? A mutual fund is both an investment vehicle and an investment strategy. Because of the different objectives and different characteristics of mutual funds, and because they are actively managed pools of money, they can be used as substitutes for stocks or bonds in the low-risk and high-risk strategies, making them an investment vehicle. Later on in this chapter we'll see how certain mutual funds can be used as strategies.

Risk Can Change

The degree of risk of a particular investment may change over time. Some investments are low risk today but may be high risk tomorrow. Example: utility stocks. Utility companies finance most of their construction through debt-issuing. Therefore, when interest rates rise substantially, their debt service — the interest they have to pay — increases, which puts a large burden on their operational cost and therefore their profits. Although utility companies are regulated by law, are stable, and pay high dividends, in time of rising interest rates their added interest obligations will adversely affect the price of their stock.

On the other hand, some investments that are high risk today may be low risk tomorrow. Example: emerging growth companies or new public corporations. These companies are generally small; they do not pay dividends; and they do not have long or stable earning histories. They are truly high risk. But if their management, products and financing are sound, their earnings as well as dividend payout will grow. In the future they will be far less risky.

In short, the risks in a specific company's stock depend on the future economy, future interest rates, and the ability of the company to compete effectively in the marketplace.

Reducing the Risk

It is possible to take a high-risk or intermediate-risk investment and make it look like a low-risk investment. This is done by limiting the downside risk, the risk of losing money. Usually, however, with the low-risk strategies, the more you limit the downside risk, the more you stand to forfeit on the upside. The desired change in the risk characteristics of an investment is effected through low-risk strategies.

It will be worth your time to read through the high-risk strategies even if you are a low-risk type. There are many strategies that allow you to limit your losses, particularly the conservative use of options.

Fred Schwed, Jr. in *Where Are the Customers' Yachts?* states: "When the market is doing well and your friends and neighbors are buying stocks, sell and put your money in the bank. The market will go higher — maybe quite a bit higher. Ignore it. Eventually there will be a recession. When it gets so bad as to arouse the politicians to make speeches, take your money out of the bank and buy stocks. The market will go lower — maybe quite a bit lower. Ignore it. This investment advice always works, but the procedure is so difficult that almost no one can do it."

I agree with all of Fred Schwed, Jr.'s quote except the "Ignore it" part. Mr. Schwed would have greatly improved on the usefulness of his advice had he included our low-risk strategies.

Each of you has taken the risk-tolerance tests in Section I. These tests measured your personal risk tolerance for price fluctuations; they also measured the degree to which you enjoy getting involved in financial matters. Some people love to trade actively and to read the financial pages in the newspapers. Some don't want to bother with strategies that involve more than a few steps. Knowing your own personality can help you to avoid strategies that will complicate your life.

For these reasons, the low-risk and high-risk strategies will be divided into two categories — active strategies and passive strategies. The passive strategies require initial implementation and periodic monitoring. Active strategies require more involvement and more steps.

Low-Risk Active Strategies

The following strategies are not mutually exclusive. That is, you need not limit yourself to one and only one strategy at a time. You can use two or more together whenever it makes sense to do so.

Strategy Number 1 — Limiting Losses

You have selected a stock that you believe will go up in the future. The current price is $25 per share. You place a market order and buy that stock (whose actual purchase price may differ ¼ to ½ point from the price your broker quoted you).

I recommend buying stocks in round lots, which are 100-share units, because it is easier to keep track of your portfolio. It is also cheaper to buy and sell round lots, since the commissions are higher on odd lots. Orders for fewer than 100 shares, or orders that are not in multiples of 100, are considered odd-lot. Therefore, an order to buy 77 shares of a given stock is an odd-lot order. If you wish to make small investments, I suggest you invest in a mutual fund.

At the same time that you buy the $25 stock, you place two other orders:

• A stop order to sell your stock at $22.50.

• A limit order to sell the same stock at some higher price, say $35. You may choose to place a limit order to sell at $30 — a 20 percent appreciation; at $35 for a 40 percent appreciation; or $50 for a 100% appreciation in price.

By placing these orders, you guarantee your maximum loss to be 10 percent of your initial investment, while ensuring that, should the price go up, you will realize the 20 percent, 40 percent, or 100 percent respectively.

If, subsequently, the price of the stock goes down 10 percent, the stock is automatically sold at $22.50. You now have $2,250 left. Have a clear understanding with your broker that any cash in your account should always be earning interest. It could be either at the broker's rate in your broker's cash account or with a money market fund that your broker is affiliated with. Let the money sit there while you do a little bit of investigating, trying to find out why the stock's price has declined.

Has anything changed at the company since the time you bought their stock? Has the stock market as a whole declined? If the market went down and the stock dropped primarily because of that, and the fundamentals of the company are still sound, you may want to place an order to buy more of the same stock at a still lower price, say another 10 percent. This will not eliminate your initial loss, but it will let you buy back cheaper shares of the stock.

If the fundamentals of the company *have* changed, then sit on your cash and watch. Do not go back into the stock unless you believe that the company's earnings prospects will improve over the next six months to one year.

If, on the other hand, the stock's price goes up, it will be sold automatically when it reaches the price of the upper limit order. You have now realized a very handsome profit. Take half of the profit, put it away in one of the safe investments, and continue to invest with the original amount plus the other half of your profits. Most importantly, don't kick yourself if the price continues to go up above the point at which you sold it. Nobody can precisely predict the highs and lows of every stock. This method ensures that you minimize your risk while giving yourself an opportunity for a very substantial return. In fact, a major study by a leading investment banking (brokerage) firm has shown that the biggest mistake to which investors are prone is their disinclination to take profits. The Rothschilds' "motto" was: "We don't want the first 20 percent or the last 20 percent — we'll take the 60 percent in the middle." The Rothschilds were famous for their successful investing. J.P. Morgan, another astute investor, when asked what he had learned about the stock market, answered that the only certainty was that the market was going to go up and that the market was going to go down. Our strategies assume just that, and are designed to ensure that you change paper profits into real profits.

Strategy Number 2 — Dollar Averaging

Dollar averaging is a strategy that increases your chance of winning in the long run without having to correctly guess the direction of the market.

There are many methods of dollar averaging, and although on the surface they seem alike, they are quite different. The first method helps you to reduce the average cost of your shares. Assume you own 100 shares of stock at an initial price of $20 per share and the price subsequently drops to $16 a share. At this point, if you buy an additional 100 shares, the average cost of the 200 shares becomes $18 per share.

The price of the stock has only to rise above the average cost of $18 for you to make a profit. Had you not bought an additional 100 shares, the price would have had to rise to above $20 a share for you to make a profit. Dollar averaging works well if the fundamentals of the company have not changed and the stock is likely to go up again in the future. If the company is a deteriorating one, this strategy will be akin to throwing good money after bad. This is where a little research really pays off.

The second method of dollar cost averaging involves regular investment plans such as the ones that mutual funds offer. It involves investing a fixed amount of money at regular intervals such as every month or every three months. When the market is down, you are buying more units or more shares with your money because of the lower cost per share. When the market is up, you are buying fewer shares at the higher cost per share. This way, you end up owning fewer of the higher cost shares and more of the lower cost shares. This brings your average cost down. Keep in mind that this method works best during markets that are on a long-term up trend. That doesn't mean simply that the market goes up, but that each consecutive peak of the cycle is higher than the previous peak, which has been the case of most of the markets from 1927 on, with the exception of the 1973-1976 market cycle. Nineteen seventy-three and 1974 were down market years; 1975-1976 were up market years. But the high of 1976 was lower than the high of 1972.

Low-Risk Passive Strategy

Low-risk passive strategies do not require a lot of buying and selling. They are established for the long run. But just as "low risk" is subjective, so is "long run." Depending on your age and your present and future need for money, the long run can range from three to five years to twenty years.

The buy-and-hold strategy consists of buying a security and holding on to it. You might, for example, choose a high dividend- or income-producing mutual fund and hold it for the long term (ten to twenty years). This may be a mutual bond fund or a conservative high-income common stock mutual fund. Although this strategy is simple, your primary risk is buying at the wrong time.

Assume that the market fluctuates as follows:

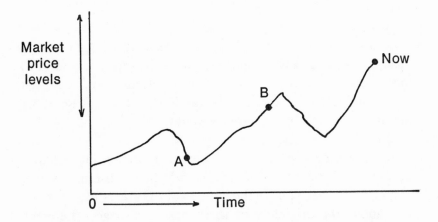

You can see that buying and holding a stock or a mutual fund at point A would provide you with much higher returns than buying the stock at point B. Using active strategies that involve more frequent trading can reduce the risk of buying at the wrong time, although these strategies may not be secure enough for low-risk types.

Inflation Hedges

Inflation hedges are just that — hedges against inflation. If high inflation continues or increases, these investments are likely to continue to appreciate in value. However, if inflation slows down or declines, they may not appreciate and may even decline in value.

Real Estate

Investing in a first home, and perhaps in a second (vacation) home, has been one of the best ways to stay ahead of inflation, because real estate can work for you in all of the following ways:

Price appreciation. In the past, housing prices have tended to go up considerably faster than the rate of inflation. They are likely to continue to do so as long as high inflation continues.

Leverage. Generally people buy houses by making a down payment of 10 to 25 percent and borrowing the rest in the form of a mortgage. The two examples below illustrate how buying your own home and/or a second vacation home is truly a case of making other people's money work for you.

Tax advantages. All property taxes and mortgage interest are tax deductible. These breaks alone can give you a substantial savings. In addition, when you sell the house, your profit — the return over and above the original purchase price — also gets preferential treatment since it is taxed as a capital gain: only 40 percent of the profit is taxed. Still another tax benefit is the once-in-a-lifetime $125,000 exclusion from taxation which can be taken after age fifty-five. Also, if you reinvest the proceeds of the sale of your home in another property within eighteen months of the sale, these proceeds are not taxed.

Why Do Real Estate Prices Fluctuate?

In the short term, housing prices tend to drop when mortgage money is scarce or interest rates are high. Sellers must usually lower their prices in order to make the property attractive enough to compensate for tight or expensive mortgage money. It generally takes about three months to sell a house, but in a period of tight or expensive mortgage money, you may have to wait six months to a year for the right buyer to come along. Those who buy a house during a time of scarce, expensive mortgage money hoping for a capital gain or for quick profit at resale may be very disappointed.

Cash Flow

Prospective buyers must also consider their cash flow. Even though homes provide substantial tax savings as well as the potential for price appreciation and even income, you must still have sufficient cash for day-to-day living expenses, taxes and mortgage payments. Buying a home is not a sound investment if the owners are left "house poor," meaning they are destitute after meeting the monthly payments on their house. Potential buyers must make sure that they have enough income each month not only to meet their payments but also to cover their other daily needs and expenses.

Another pitfall of buying a house has to do with the two-income family. By law, a bank or lending institution must include both incomes when it evaluates a mortgage application. And many couples assume they will have a dual income for many years. But if at some point the wife becomes pregnant, she may want to stop working. Even if she continues to work, the child becomes an added expense in the family budget. Every potential house buyer really needs enough monthly income to finance not only the house, but also the unexpected.

In addition to financial considerations, there are some others. Maintenance and upkeep of the house and property become your direct responsibilities (unless you purchase a cooperative apartment). When anything needs to be repaired (furnace, pipes, roof, etc.), *you* have to take care of it. There is no landlord or superintendent to depend on.

Aside from these crucial considerations, owning a home produces benefits far beyond just having a roof over your head.

Buying Your First Home

Linda and Gary Smith, a young couple with a joint income of $3,000 a month, found a house priced at $80,000. The location, the size, and the style fit their every dream, and they decided to buy. Using $10,000 from their savings and a $10,000 loan from their parents for the 25 percent down payment, they took out a $60,000 mortgage at 15 percent.

During this first year of their ownership of the house, it has cost them a substantial portion of their $36,000 annual income. Their mortgage payments alone come to $981 a month, nearly half their monthly take-home pay. Utilities, heating and maintenance, and taxes added another $400 per month to their payout. The interest on the borrowed part of the down payment adds another $150 a month. Linda and Gary spend almost $2 out of every $3 they earn for the house. Keep in mind, though, that the interest on the mortgage (which in the early years is almost the entire payment) and the property taxes are fully tax deductible. The Smiths, however, will not realize this benefit until tax time. It has not helped their cash flow during the year.

There is no doubt that this payment pattern is a hefty burden for a young couple starting out. They are paying very valuable dollars for their little dream house. But let's look five years into the future.

If Gary and Linda are like most couples, their incomes will rise in real terms at a rate of about 5 percent annually between the ages of thirty and thirty-five. Assuming a 10 percent annual rate of inflation, their nominal incomes should rise about 15 percent every year. In five years, assuming they both continue to work, their monthly income will have reached about $6,000 a month. *But the monthly payout for the house will remain more or less fixed.* Now they will be paying out about $1 in $4 of their income for this house. In ten years, they will only be spending about $1 out of $12 for the same house.

If house prices continue to rise, the value of the Smiths' home will have grown appreciably. Gary and Linda will not realize this price appreciation, of course, until they sell the house; but, because of inflation, they are paying off the house in cheaper dollars, and in five years the house could be worth $160,000 — an appreciation of $80,000 over the price they paid.

But they are actually even better off than that. Linda and Gary put down only $10,000 of their own money to buy that house. The $80,000 appreciation, therefore, represents an 800 percent increase on their own investment. They were using the bank's money and their parents' money to make money for themselves.

Mortgages

Gary and Linda hold a conventional 25-year fixed-payment mortgage. Because of current high interest rates, a myriad of new mortgage types have become available. Most of them are designed to help people buy today's expensive houses at today's high interest rates. The idea is to reduce monthly payments during the early years when a young couple's income is not so high.

Until the last few years, a mortgage was a simple low-cost, fixed-rate, thirty-year loan. Such a loan allowed your parents or your grandparents to own and to profit from owning their own homes.

Today, mortgages are different. Because of high interest rates (17 to 19 percent) on the traditional mortgages, most people could not afford the "old-fashioned" mortgage, and probably would not even qualify for one.

What do these people do? They use the new creative financing techniques. Creative financing is a term that covers a large number of new types of mortgages and payment schemes, all designed to reduce the monthly payments for the buyer without the seller's having to reduce the selling price of a house. There are many types of new financing arrangements, and the number is growing every day. Creative financing has shifted the burden of inflation and economic instability from the lending institution onto the consumer. Financial institutions are no longer willing to assume the risks involved in committing their own funds to a thirty-year fixed-rate loan.

Three years ago creative financing accounted for 10 to 15 percent of house sales. Today it is the basis of 80 percent of all housing transactions.

But what exactly *is* creative financing? It is simply a scheme to reduce the monthly payments on a mortgage. Some of the most frequently used methods are:

Graduated-payment. These mortgages cost less in the early years when the holder makes less money; payments increase in later years when presumably he earns more.

To illustrate, Gary and Linda are paying $981 a month for their mortgage over a twenty-five-year period. Under a graduated-payment mortgage, their payment schedule might look like this:

Years one to five .... $600 per month
Years six to ten............................. $900 per month
Years eleven to twenty-five .... $1,300 per month

While graduated-payment mortgages cost more than conventional mortgages, they help you to pay back fewer of the expensive dollars and more of the cheap dollars.

Shared-appreciation. These mortgages give the mortgage issuer (the bank, the seller, the developer) the right to share in the appreciation of the house when it is sold. The amount that is "shared" generally varies from 25 to 50 percent of the increased value of the house. The lender (issuer) may, for example, contract for 30 percent of the appreciation value. For this right, the 30 percent share in the appreciation of the house, the lender accepts lower monthly payments, or a lower rate of interest. However, when the house is sold, 30 percent of the appreciation goes to the mortgage lender. If Linda and Gary had taken a 30 percent shared-appreciation mortgage, their monthly payment would have been about $680, a savings of about $300 a month over their conventional mortgage. But if five years later they sold the house for $160,000, the mortgage holder would claim 30 percent of the $80,000 profit, or $24,000.

Although this arrangement cuts into the owner's profit potential in the house, it does help young couples starting out to buy the house they want.

Variable rate. The payments on these mortgages vary according to prevailing interest rates. This method may be a boon to current home buyers, since interest rates are on the decline, but it has been a catastrophe for those homeowners who got such a mortgage five years ago when mortgages were at 8 to 9 percent. Some of those people have seen their monthly payments more than double in the last two or three years.

Renegotiable. The interest rates on these mortgages are re-negotiated periodically. The intervals can vary from one to five years.

Contract for deed. If the buyer cannot arrange enough financing to cover the entire purchase price, he contracts with the seller to pay the down payment at some point in the future. Interest on this amount can be paid monthly or added to the total amount due at the end (the balloon payment). The deed to the house remains in the name of the original owner (the seller) until the down payment plus interest is paid.

Negative amortizer. The buyer gets a mortgage at a reduced interest rate, but the difference between that rate and the prevailing interest rate is added to the principal. Monthly payments are gradually increased as the amount of the principal increases.

These are just a few of the mortgages. Others include the "balloon mortgage," the "wraparound," the "equity participator." Even though these terms are becoming accepted, they may mean different things to different people. The terms and conditions will also vary in most cases. And there are as many combinations and permutations in creative financing as there are creative people.

When deciding what financing arrangements are right for you, the most important things to keep in mind are:

1. Will I be able to afford future payments? This is particularly important in the case of a contract for deed, or of a balloon mortgage, where a large lump sum is due at some point in the future. Foreclosures are currently up more than 100 percent over last year's total.

2. What is the real cost of this financing? Good real estate strategy assumes that you know your costs and that you make sure the price appreciation and/or the income from the property exceeds those costs.

Generally, as interest rates rise, real estate values decline; and when interest rates decline, prices go up.

One further point about owning your first home. Never forget that buying and selling houses is not a liquid transaction. In other words, you cannot sell a house instantaneously. But as long as you buy it to live in, rather than for speculation, it pays to make the smallest possible down payment. The smaller the down payment, the larger the mortgage; the larger the mortgage, the higher the monthly payments; but in most cases the higher the monthly payments, the greater the opportunity of a high return on the initial investment or down payment.

Buying a Second Home or Vacation Home

Linda and Gary have now lived in their home for five years and are quite happy there. But they also vacation each year at a popular ski resort and are tired of the crowded impersonality of a hotel. "A condominium at the resort would be so nice," they tell each other.

Yes, it would be; but before they actually purchase one, they must do some basic thinking. Linda and Gary already have a home, the one in which they live. They cannot possibly live in a second house or even use the second house for more than a few weeks and weekends a year. This would leave their condominium available for rental much of the time. This is crucial, because without some rental income from the second home, the Smiths probably would not be able to meet their monthly payment on two homes at the same time. In fact, their major consideration in buying a second home or condominium is whether the new property can and will produce income.

Good rental properties are usually located near a seasonal recreation area: on the beaches along the Florida coast; on the ski slopes of Aspen, Jackson Hole or Vail; or in the mountains of northern Vermont, New Hampshire, or Massachusetts. Ideally, rental properties should be located in places that attract winter as well as summer trade.

After shopping around for several months, the Smiths find a

two-bedroom condominium in the resort town where they ski. They sit down with a local real estate agent who tells them that, given a good skiing season, they can expect to rent their condominium for one hundred twenty days out of the year. During a bad year, they may still be able to rent it for sixty days. In addition to the "winter trade," this resort also has summer recreational facilities. In other words, it has a year-round possibility of generating rental income.

The condominium that Gary and Linda find at their ski resort sells for $60,000. Their down payment is $15,000, or 25 percent of the purchase price. They will have to finance the rest.

In order to make the down payment, the Smiths decided to refinance their first home. They do this by going to a local bank (although they could have gone to a second-mortgage company) and taking a second mortgage on their first home in the amount of $15,000. In fact, the Smiths could have borrowed up to $64,000 on a second mortgage (80 percent of the price appreciation) if the rates had been more favorable than on a brand-new mortgage.

Gary and Linda now own a second home with a $45,000 mortgage. They pay 15 percent a year on this loan, or about $600 a month. They rent the condominium for the maximum period they can. In a very good year that means one hundred twenty days at $75 a day, or $9,000. While this sum sounds large, Gary and Linda have expenses over and above their monthly payments, as they do on their first home. Add to these maintenance, taxes, and commissions to the rental agent. Even after they deduct these costs from their income tax, Gary and Linda may have a loss in terms of cash flow. That is, their "out of pocket" expenses may still exceed their rental income in any one year.

Yet their condominium will probably appreciate in value. It may appreciate by 15 percent a year or more. The Smiths bought this house without putting down any of their own money — they had borrowed the entire down payment. When at some future date they decide to sell it or borrow against it, the proceeds will be "free and clear."

The possibility of additional future profit also exists, because the rent they charge can be increased as time passes. In a few years they may be able to rent their condominium for $100 a day or more. Gary and Linda will then have a real cash-flow profit on top of any profit they may get from price appreciation. Of course, the same logic applies for each additional house — third, fourth, and fifth — bought with the idea of getting extra returns.

Most of the calculations that go into buying a second house with rental income can be applied to the purchase of a combination residence and rental property. An income-producing rental property may be a two-family house where one unit is available for rental, or an apartment house with several rental units.

Do keep in mind, however, that a reliable cash flow is necessary to finance such ventures, particularly if you wish to make capital improvements. Capital improvements on the property will probably generate appreciation far in excess of the dollar investment, yet the investor must be able to pay for them when the work is done. Nobody wants to find himself in a situation where a bank or second-mortgage company can repossess any of these properties.

As we mentioned earlier, profits from the sale are tax-free if they are reinvested in real estate within eighteen months of the sale date. If the profits are not reinvested in real estate, they are fully taxed as ordinary income — with one exception: after the age of fifty-five there is a once-in-a-lifetime exemption of the first $125,000 in profit from the sale of a house.

The profit potential of owning a first home or a second or third income-producing property is great. But don't forget the disadvantages. Owner-landlords have responsibility for maintaining the property. This involves supplying heat, gas, and electricity. It also means carrying insurance, paying for repairs and upkeep, and taking care that the property looks good. Property that is not kept up may decrease in value. Remember that real estate is an inflation hedge. When inflation is on the rise, property values usually increase. When money is tight or inflation is low, real estate values may decrease.

Collectibles

If after all of the warnings in the previous section you are still interested in collectibles, I suggest the following guidelines. First, invest money in a collectible only if you are willing to treat it as a hobby and to spend time and effort to shop, appraise, evaluate, talk to experts, and read everything you can about your collection.

Second, invest only if you can afford to buy items of top quality. Unless you invest in the finest quality collectibles, you have a very slim chance of making as much money as you could from a safe investment such as a bond or a certificate of deposit.

Third, invest in collectibles only if you are willing and able to hold on to them for long periods of time. Because commissions, sales taxes, storage fees, and insurance add to the cost of a collectible, the value of an item may have to double for you just to break even. And the collection or item should always be insured for its current replacement value — the cost of replacing the item should it be lost, stolen, damaged or destroyed.

Finally, trade only with the most reputable dealers. Make sure to check references and sources. Stay away from those who offer to sell something but cannot or will not give information about its background. It is always better to be suspicious and lose out on a true bargain than to be trusting and be cheated. Whenever possible, get the dealer to agree to a "buy-back" agreement. Such an agreement ensures that the dealer will buy the item back from you within a stated period of time and for a prestated price.

To conclude, unless you are an expert or are willing to become one, leave investing in collectibles to the experts; in other words, the strategy is to become an expert yourself.

High-Risk Strategies

By our previous definition, high-risk strategies refer to those in which the investor uses leverage or invests in very risky assets. I have explained earlier how leveraged investment strategies can produce losses far beyond your original investment. In this section, however, we will discuss only those strategies in which the maximum possible loss is limited to the amount of your investment. The one exception is real estate.

Real Estate

Earlier we categorized real estate as an inflation hedge. But there are times when an inflation hedge may act like a high-risk investment.

The average investor has several ways, both direct and indirect, to invest money in real estate. The direct way is actual possession or ownership of a property. Indirect ways include buying into Real Estate Investment Trusts (REIT), which pool many mortgages; or buying a Government National Mortgage Association bond (GNMA, or "Ginnie Mae" as it is affectionately known on Wall Street); or purchasing a Federal Mortgage Acceptance Corporation bond (known as Freddie Mac). All of these vehicles are simply pools of mortgages which are owned by these agencies or trusts. As for the direct methods, the major categories are:

1. Buying and owning a home to live in.

2. Buying land to build on at a later date or for speculators.

3. Buying properties that generate income, such as a multifamily dwelling.

Buying a home to live in. When you buy a home, it becomes the least liquid of investments. Although there is always a market price at which you might sell it, a death in the family, relocation, or a transfer may force you to sell it at somewhat less than the ideal time. Therein lies the risk.

Traditionally, the housing market has gone up at a rate faster than inflation over the long run; in the short run, however, there have been periods of price decline. Because prices have steadily risen without the usual declines in the past decade, many investors may feel that this trend will continue, but the current high cost of financing could cause a decline in the housing market. In fact, certain parts of the country have already experienced a decline.

No one is currently predicting a drop of 75 or even 50 percent. Twenty percent is more likely over the next few years. Any decline, though, poses a risk for the homeowner, the risk of having to sell during this decline.

Anyone buying a home today usually puts down between 20 and 25 percent. Assume you just bought a home with a 25 percent down payment. Two years hence, housing prices drop 25 percent and your firm transfers you to another part of the country. You put your house up for sale. Because the market has declined by 25 percent and you put down 25 percent originally, you have risked your total initial investment.

Many corporations, aware of the risk involved in buying and selling homes, offer a transferred employee the differential when he is obliged to sell his home for less than he paid for it. If you have such an agreement with your employer, the risk is eliminated.

Buying undeveloped land. Undeveloped land is purchased for speculative purposes or for construction at a later date. Land prices have gone up much faster than housing prices. And, in a sense, land can be considered a very leveraged investment that offers great potential rewards. But unimproved or undeveloped property does not produce income and yet does incur costs such as mortgage payments and taxes. This means that as long as you hold the land, you have cash outflow but no cash inflow.

Given these characteristics, land, in particular unimproved land, can be a very profitable investment, but calculate your total costs before investing. Furthermore, be prepared to hold the property for several years. The longer you hold unimproved real estate, the less likely you are to lose money on resale. There are always periodic declines, but you can weather them if you do not have to sell the land.

Investing in rental property. In most cases, the income from a multifamily dwelling offsets the cost of operating it; in some cases you may even have money left over, and virtually all expenses associated with such a building are tax deductible.

Again, this may turn out to be a great opportunity, and your risk is low because your cash outflow is generally protected by the cash inflow from the tenants. This type of investment does, however, require your attention. Repairs must be made to the building, the sidewalks, the boiler, the roof; any and all complaints must be answered; rent must be collected, tenants screened, and so forth. Unless you can afford to hire a superintendent or manager for the building, your investment, though profitable, can be time consuming. Weigh this fact very carefully before you become a landlord.

Securities

High-risk investments may also include high-risk stocks or bonds. A typical high-risk bond is a low-quality, long-maturity deep-discount bond; for example, a bbb-rated bond with a twenty-year maturity and a 6 percent coupon selling at $31 ($310 per bond). A typical high-risk stock is one issued by a fledgling company or a company that has recently had serious earnings or profit problems.

High-Risk Active Strategies

All the low-risk strategies can be turned into high-risk strategies given the addition of two conditions:

1. The use of margin or leverage.

2. The selection of stocks or bonds that are volatile and therefore risky.

In regard to item 1, you can leverage your investments by using a broker margin account to borrow on the value of your securities, or to borrow from any other source and then to invest the entire amount.

High-Risk Passive Strategies

Closed-End Mutual Funds

Open-end mutual funds trade at their net asset value (NAV) for no-load funds, and at NAV plus the load (salesman's commission) for load funds. A closed-end fund, however, may trade at a discount or premium from its net asset value. Recently, most closed-end funds have been trading at a discount from NAV, their average market value. In up markets, the amount of the discount decreases and the fund may trade at a premium. In down markets, the discount may get larger.

When you buy a closed end at an historically high discount, you are getting free leverage. For example: Fund A has a NAV of $25 a share. However, it is currently selling at $20, a discount of 20 percent. If the NAV of the fund goes to $40 a share, the price may go up to $38, reducing the discount to 5 percent. You, the investor, had a return of 90 percent ([$38 – $20] ÷ $20), even though the NAV increased by only 60 percent ([$40 – $25] ÷ $25). You benefited both by the price appreciation and by the free leverage of the reduction in the discount.

When the NAV rises to $40, demand for shares may increase. Since a closed-end fund does not issue new shares, investors may bid up the price to $44 a share — a 10 percent premium. In that case, your return will be 120 percent even though the increase in the NAV is still 60 percent. The 20 percent discount has become a 10 percent premium.

High-Risk Strategy — Options

When I was planning this book, options caused a bit of a dilemma. "Where," I wondered, "do they belong?" The average investor may argue that "They're risky, so they should be categorized in high risk." Options can be used speculatively, but they can also be used conservatively — to lock in a price appreciation, or increase the income you can generate on a stock you now own. I finally arrived at a compromise. I placed the subject of options under high risk, but I discuss the buying and selling of options in both ways.

Conservative Use of Options

Using call options to increase your income. You own ABC stock currently at $40 a share. You may sell a call option contract at $3 a share, which gives an investor the right to buy the ABC stock from you at $45 a share within three months. If the price does *not* reach $45, you have an additional income of $300 from selling the option ($3 a share for a 100-share contract).

If, however, the price goes to $50, the ABC stock will be purchased away from you at $45 a share. You have earned $8 a share, $5 from the price appreciation and $3 from the sale of the option. You could have made $10 a share had you not written a call option — a safe bet but a conservative one.

Yes, a bet.

When you write (sell) a covered call option, you are betting that the price will not exceed the strike price plus the income from the option. You are also increasing your income if the stock is not called away from you.

Another advantage to writing covered call options is that it forces you to realize your profit on price appreciation. So make sure you can live with the profit at the strike price.

Using puts to reduce risk. A while ago you bought 100 shares of ABC stock at $30. It went up to $45 and is now at $40. You can buy a put option (say for $2 a share) to sell the stock at $40 in order to lock in most of your profit. If, subsequently, the ABC stock declines in price to $35 a share, you can sell it for $40. Since the put option cost you $2 a share, your real price is $38 a share minus commissions. You have locked in about $8 a share in profit.

Straddles allow you to benefit from large price fluctuations. The straddle strategy involves simultaneous buying and selling, a combination of a put and a call option on the same stock. These put and call options will also have the same strike price and the same expiration date. By purchasing a straddle you can benefit from either a substantial rise or a decline in the price of the stock. One option will become worthless, whereas the other will appreciate. However, the price movements, whether up or down, must exceed the cost of the straddle in order for you to make a profit. If the underlying stock's price has not changed, you will lose the entire cost of the option.

Options — Aggressive Strategies

Buying call options. You buy a call option when you think that a stock will greatly appreciate in value within the term of the option contract. If it does rise in price, you will have a much greater appreciation in the option than you would have had in the stock itself.

If the price of the stock declines, the option will lose much of its value, or even become worthless. Since options fluctuate greatly in price, putting a stop-sell order at 10 percent below your cost will almost guarantee that it will be sold at a loss. You may, however, want to sell the option if the price of the underlying stock begins to decline quickly, or you may put in a stop order at 50 percent below your cost.

Buying "naked" (uncovered put) options allows you to capitalize on a price decline. If you believe a stock will fall in value within a short time, you may gain from that decline by "shorting" it. Shorting a stock means selling it at today's price for delivery at some future date. If the price falls as expected, you buy it at the lower price and deliver it at the higher pre-agreed price. You keep the difference. Of course, if the price increases, you have to buy the more expensive shares and deliver them at a loss.

Buying a naked put option accomplishes the same thing, but it is cheaper, much more leveraged, and potentially much more profitable.

In order to protect yourself from losses, simultaneously with buying a put option, you may want to place an order to buy the stock should it begin to rise in price. Your uncovered (naked) option is now partially covered.

When using aggressive options strategies, follow the prices of the stock and the option very closely. If something seems to be going wrong, get ready to sell quickly. These strategies are not for the fainthearted or for procrastinators. Option markets have many more losers than winners. But when you win, you can win big.

Paper Portfolio Strategy

One further note . . . we have gotten into strategies that involve risk in varying degrees. If you feel a bit "gun-shy," you can try these strategies on paper first. To do so, select the strategy that most appeals to you, pretend you have bought the bonds, stocks or options, and keep track of what happens. This helps many people overcome their fear of investing and clarifies the details and procedures. If you strike it rich on paper, though, you cannot spend the rewards, but you can sure tell your friends and neighbors about your score!

In Conclusion . . .

This book may not make you rich, but it can provide you with thousands and even tens of thousands of dollars in additional earnings or cost savings.

It will also help you plan for your future, by giving you a solid foundation on which to assess what you have, what you *can* have, and how to get it!

INDEX